Sam Makhoul

A Higher
Branch

What if happiness is as simple
as climbing higher?

A Higher Branch
International Pty Limited

First published in 2011 by
A Higher Branch International Pty Limited

ABN 52 144 693 550

Suite 212, 43 Majors Bay Road
Concord 2137, Sydney
New South Wales
Australia

Copyright © Sam Makhoul 2011

Sam Makhoul asserts the moral right to be identified as the author of this work.

Illustrations copyright © Richard Hayes and David Oberdorf 2011

Cover design by the Modern Art Production Company

Typeset in 11pt/15pt ITC Garamond Light by Prototype Pty Ltd.

National Library of Australia
Cataloguing in Print Data
    A Higher Branch
    ISBN: 978-0 9870618-1-2
    Makhoul, Sam

    A Higher Branch: What if happiness is as simple as climbing higher?/
    Sam Makhoul
    2nd Edition
    Dewey Number: A823.4

The author is grateful for permission by Pollinger Limited, Author's Agents, UK to use the following previously copyrighted material 'Wandering' by Hermann Hesse.

This book is dedicated to my grandmother Rose Makhoul.
It was on her mulberry tree that I reached for my first branch.
She made my childhood magical, during what were
turbulent times in Lebanon's history.

And to my children Christopher, Matthew and Amelia,
without whom I cannot breathe.

Contents

FOREWORD

This book is a guide to life, a journal and an inspiring story – almost a novel. It is a magical journey filled with beautiful analogies that are sure to live in your memory long after you have read it.

For as long as I have known Sam he has travelled through life with a journal in his hands and his eyes firmly fixed on achievement. Not content with standing still, he has a childlike excitement for the future and all its possibilities.

Sam is a dreamer, a thinker, an idealist, a student of life and a person with a curiosity for other people's potential. He is also an entrepreneur at heart but one with a keen sense of justice and a love for humanity.

Sam has written this fable with deliberate simplicity. He likes to write as he speaks, freely and spontaneously. He uses the language of life that leaves no reader behind.

Katrina Makhoul

Prologue

We Are All Born to Climb

Simply by observing children playing, you will notice a strong urge to climb. They love to climb everything from trees in the park, to monkey bars, backs of adults and just about anything that sees them reaching higher off the ground.

So what is it about climbing that makes it so alluring?

On a recent visit to a playground in a local park, my six-year-old daughter reminded me of my own love for climbing. Instead of running to the swings, as she usually does, she decided to detour and start climbing a magnificent Moreton Bay fig tree.

Naturally as a parent, my first reaction was to stop her from getting too high. Despite my repeated requests for her to come down, she persisted fearlessly. Never wanting to teach my children to fear, I decided to climb with her, to help her get a better grip and to ensure she did not fall. As I reached her, she decided to climb even higher. I was intrigued by her fascination to climb for no apparent reason, except to get to the next branch.

I finally had her attention and asked, "Sweetie, why do you want to keep climbing?" She looked down at me with the sparkle of adventure in her eyes and replied, "Because I want to climb to a higher branch, Daddy." In that instant, a sense of déjà vu tunnelled through my memory and reacquainted me with a wisdom that I had been unwittingly living by all my life. I stood there and saw myself on a similar branch thirty-eight years earlier.

So it was on that sunny afternoon in a modest Sydney park that my daughter reconnected me with the most magical time of my childhood. Watching her climb triggered a series of memories that had been locked in my subconscious. They were fond recollections of an eight-year-old boy, lying in the shade of a fig tree in his grandmother's orchard, looking up at the sun through rustling leaves. There was also the memory of that same strong urge to climb each and every tree in that orchard. Most of all, I recalled a *feeling* that you only get when you climb to a higher branch. A feeling of freedom, combined with strength and a sense of achievement. It was also a sentiment of deep wisdom that can only be found when we connect with trees.

> *"Trees are sanctuaries. Whoever knows how to speak to them, whoever knows how to listen to them, can learn the truth. They do not preach learning or precepts, they preach, undeterred by particulars, the ancient law of life."*

– Hermann Hesse, 'Wandering'

Later that day, my daughter and I went home and sat on the grass in the backyard. As she played with her toys, I sat next to her with my journal in one hand and a pen in the other, contemplating what I had just experienced.

I looked back on my life and realised that while I had loved climbing trees as a boy, metaphorically speaking, I never stopped climbing as an adult. I realised that the act of reaching and climbing had helped me through adolescence, it had helped me through school and university, it had helped me in my relationships and it had helped me throughout my career. All in all, the simple act of climbing had helped me to live *my* best life.

That same afternoon, I began writing this book.

A Higher Branch began as an odyssey to relive my childhood, but it quickly turned into so much more. I soon realised that the urge to climb higher had shaped my whole life, by giving me a guide and a powerful pattern of thinking that hard-wired me for achievement.

I began to feel grateful to have lived by the wisdom. At the same time, it seemed somewhat selfish to have kept it to myself all these years. I felt the need to share it with others – my children, my family, my friends and my work colleagues.

Injustice

Many years ago, I became a lawyer because I hated injustice. I always thought of injustice as something that is thrust upon us. But as I grew older, I discovered that the biggest injustice in people's lives was the one they dealt themselves by not living to their full potential. It is an injustice not only to themselves but to their families who do not get to see them at their best. More so, it is an injustice to the world that does not get to witness their brilliance.

I am a firm believer that we are all born with a talent that is unique to us; that we all have something special to show the world. With this in mind, I have lived with a curiosity for why many people go through life without ever reaching that potential.

There is no doubt that most of us do not climb because we fear. We fear falling. We fear getting hurt. But I have also realised that there is something other than fear that keeps us from climbing to the level of extraordinary – our circumstances.

My Story

In my country of birth, Lebanon, my parents had a very easy lifestyle. My father worked in an executive position managing a luxury hotel in Beirut. His job took him to many exotic locations throughout Europe and the Middle East, coordinating events for royal families and other dignitaries. He spoke five languages. My mother raised us with the help of a nanny and a housemaid. She spent most days having coffee with friends and pampering herself in a beauty salon.

This lifestyle was shattered on one ordinary day in October 1973. I recall my parents turning up to school with a distressed look on their faces to collect my brother and I from class. I remember hearing unfamiliar loud noises in the background; it was the noise of anger and artillery. I remember the frantic drive home and the dash from the car to the lobby that took us up to our apartment. I remember my parents hurriedly collecting our belongings. Tanks and soldiers were barraging down the street as we left. I did not realise that I would be leaving my home for the last time.

Twenty-four hours later, my family and I were transported to a foreign country, the great southern land of Australia. My parents, a façade of bravery. My face, filled with enthusiasm for meeting new friends. I was told that the people looked different, ate different food and loved sport. That the land was flat and the beaches sandy. I could not contain my excitement.

To a boy, Australia was a part of mother Earth, a place to call home and a chance to connect with new people. Their differences made me curious and made me feel more alive with anticipation. I now believe that it is truly our curiosity to know more about our differences that should bring us together, not tear us apart.

In Australia, my parents learned to let go of their comfortable lifestyle and took on any job that was available. They were strong and industrious. They struggled with the language, felt isolated and often fell ill from being overworked. But they never stopped climbing.

I share this story with you to demonstrate the point that no one is born into a perfect set of circumstances. I certainly experienced a number of struggles and setbacks throughout my life, most of which were thrust upon me. Like many, I also lived with fears and insecurities. But despite these challenges, I have been blessed with a life full of love, contentment and purpose.

More than I ever imagined possible. Why? The answer is simple, and it was revealed to me on that sunny spring afternoon when my daughter climbed a tree and looked down on me with a face so full of excitement that you would think she had discovered a pot of gold at the end of a rainbow.

You see, like myself, my daughter had discovered the wisdom of climbing to a higher branch.

When you climb, you achieve. When you stop climbing, you stagnate. Eating the fruit on the highest branch is not what brings ultimate satisfaction. Sure, it gives you a brief sense of achievement, but it is the simple act of constant climbing that gives you meaning and lasting happiness. You will continue to grow as you climb higher. If you stop climbing however, you will cease to grow. When that happens, you may start to feel despondent. What most people call depression is sometimes nothing more than stagnation of the human spirit. This affliction does not discriminate. Whether you are rich or poor, upper class or middle class, third world or first world, if you cease to climb higher, you will lose your way in life. If, however, you choose to keep climbing, happiness will not discriminate either. You will experience happiness no matter your circumstances.

I humbly share this story with you, in the hope that it will change your life, like it did mine.

THE
STREAM

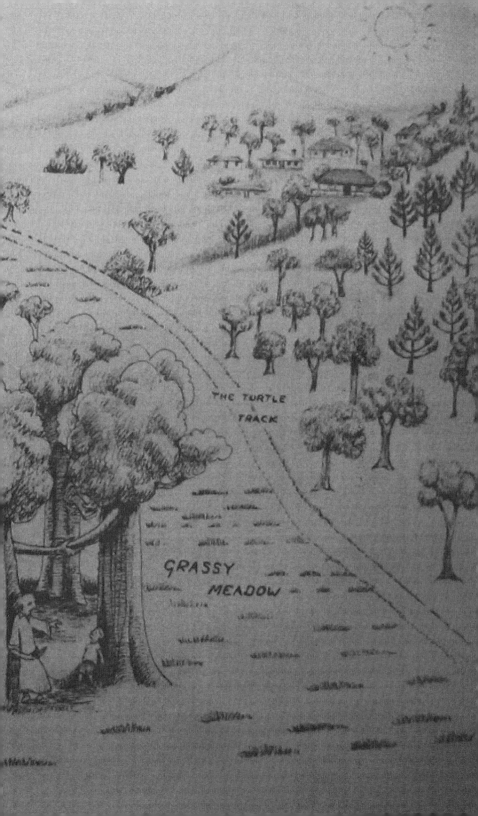

THE TURTLE TRACK

GRASSY MEADOW

Part One

THE EIGHT TREES
OF LIFE

CHAPTER 1

The Boy who Loves to Climb

*"Each child is an adventure
into a better life – an opportunity to change
the old pattern and make it new."*

Hubert H. Humphrey

When I was eight years old, I had one of those life-changing experiences that some people talk of when they are much older, perhaps as a result of an epiphany or a life-altering illness. My memory of it is so vivid that I am able to write about it many years after it happened. It shapes my thinking and dictates every decision I make in life.

My story begins on one sunny afternoon, when I ventured away from home to explore the woods. It was a serene time of the day with no clouds in the sky and a stillness made for daydreaming. The sound of birds searching for a spot to settle, filled the air.

I was a boy like any other, curious and adventurous. I loved being surrounded by nature. I loved walking past the trees with my head constantly looking up in search of interesting happenings that took place in them.

As I wandered through the woods on that day, I came across a tree that I hadn't seen before. It was larger than any other. It was strange that I hadn't noticed it on my previous treks. How could I have missed it? I knew the woods like the back of my hand.

My eyes scanned the breadth of the tree and I noticed something odd about it. Its leaves were rustling, even though there was no wind blowing. The surrounding trees were eerily still, but the branches of this tree moved like it was beckoning me to get closer to it. To touch it. To climb it.

I approached cautiously and could not help but feel a connection. I ran the palm of my hand over the bark and looked up at the fork in the trunk where the branches fan out into all different directions. I noticed that the tree was high and difficult to climb, but that did not deter me. I used the knots in the trunk for leverage to start my climb. They were deeply embedded and seemed to be located in just the right spots. As I placed my hand on the first knot, it strangely felt like the strong supportive hand of my father.

I started climbing with the fearless determination that only a child could muster. After I worked my way up to the top of the trunk, I started reaching for the many branches that were on offer, slowly getting higher and higher until I was at the very top canopy. I stood there, perched for what seemed like a long time and admired the tree's detailed and ancient structure beneath me. I felt a sense of freedom. I felt strong. I felt energetic. I felt supported.

The changing colours of the setting sun interrupted my daydream and I realised it would soon be getting dark. I climbed back down to where the branches met the top of the trunk and stood there pondering how to make it to the ground without falling and hurting myself. Contemplating my next move, I began to worry. The light of day was about to disappear and my parents would be expecting me home. I leaned back on a large branch, only intending to rest a moment. I felt a serene sense of calm as my mind drifted to other matters, as it so often did. The branch cradled my body and as I relaxed, I drifted off to sleep.

I awoke to the sound of birds chirping and glimpses of the sun rising in the distance. The woods looked unfamiliar. Did I wake up in a different place? How could that be? I looked out and noticed that the tree I lay in was in the middle of a meadow of lush green grass. To my right were a number of rolling hills that trailed in a row all the way to the ocean. I sat up and noticed that I was in a large majestic tree that had an elegant network of branches full of bright green foliage that appeared to be shining magically.

Around me were seven other trees with a similar network of branches. They were linked in a perfect circle, with their branches overlapping. It looked like they were holding hands and reminded me of the nursery rhyme 'ring-around-the-rosie'.

Was I in a dream or did I sleepwalk to another meadow? And how could it be the morning? The sun was setting when I drifted off to sleep. Did I spend the whole night on the tree?

I will never know whether what happened next was a dream or not. What I do know is that it changed my life forever.

I heard water trickling at the base of the trunk and looked down to see an old man dressed in bright white clothing with a watering can in one hand. He appeared to be illuminated by the morning light. He looked up at me, smiled and greeted me with a warm "Hello".

"Hello," I replied hesitantly.

"Are you enjoying this tree?" he asked.

"Yes, but I need to climb down and find my way home."

"Then jump down," he suggested.

"It's too high. I'll hurt myself."

"Don't worry, I will catch you," he assured me.

I looked down cautiously at him. My parents had taught me to never talk to strangers; but he looked harmless. His soft brown eyes smiled at me. His hands were big as if they had spent their entire life working the land and his face showed an eagerness to help. Besides, I had no other option. I had to get home. I planned to make a run for it as soon as my feet touched the ground.

"Okay, here I come."

I stood up and steadied myself.

He put his watering can down and opened his arms. They appeared to stretch far and wide, as the flowing white fabric of his garment expanded like a hammock ready to catch me. I closed my eyes, jumped and felt like I had landed into a big soft pillow.

As he helped me to my feet I couldn't help but make eye contact with him. His face looked friendly and his eyes kind and gentle. There was something strangely familiar about him. I returned his smile and decided not to leave in a hurry. I was curious about what he was doing alone in the meadow.

"Why are you watering this tree?" I asked.

"I water all these eight trees daily," he replied and pointed to the trees in the circle, "but this one is my favourite. I couldn't help but notice you were sleeping peacefully on it. So I had to come over and say hello."

"Why do these eight trees look different to the other trees in the meadow?" I asked.

He looked up at them, then back at me and said, "Because these eight trees hold some very special fruit on their branches, especially this one," he gestured up to the biggest tree in the middle. "This tree holds the secret to climbing the other seven."

Before I could ask another question, the old man asked,

"Why do you love to climb?"

"I don't know," was my first response. Then I thought to myself "How does he know this?" I looked up at the trees and said, "When I reach the top, I can see everything that is happening all around me. It's like a bird's-eye view."

"Is that the only reason you like to climb?" he asked with an inquisitive smile.

"I also like the exciting feeling of climbing from branch to branch, reaching higher and higher. It's an adventure. You know, the best fruit is on the higher branches."

"Indeed it is," he said, nodding with a knowing smile.

There was a long awkward silence and my attention returned to the fact that I was lost in an unfamiliar place. I was homesick and felt weak with worry. I also felt sad because I missed my mother, father and my little sister Sophia. My dog Woody would be waiting for me at the front gate.

The old man must have sensed my concern and asked me in a gentle voice, "What is your name, son?"

"Tom," I replied.

"Well do not worry Tom. I am sure you will find your way home."

My worry subsided a little.

"Do you know where I live?" I asked with a hopeful voice.

"No, I don't, but I know how you can find your way home." He leaned over a little and added in a secretive voice, "You must first find the Garden of Happiness."

I was puzzled and asked with an equally hushed voice, "Where is that? Is it far from here?"

"It is closer than you think, Tom," he replied. "But it is what you find *in* that Garden that will lead you home."

I turned to look around the meadow. I always thought of a garden as having flowerbeds and blossoming trees, much like I would find around my grandmother's cottage. But this was not a garden I was standing in. It was a meadow with only these eight trees. They did, however, look amazing. Every time I looked at them, I felt the urge to climb. The branches looked so easy to navigate and the fruit that hung on each tree was alluring. But it was still no garden. I looked back at the old man, puzzled.

"Don't be confused, Tom. You will find what you are looking for if you follow your instinct to climb."

He leaned over again and whispered, "To find the Garden of Happiness, you must first climb these eight trees," he pointed upwards with a curious smile.

I did not understand what he meant. How could these eight trees show me the way home? Could you see my house from the top? But why would I have to climb all of them?

"Tom, the *fruit* from these eight trees will help guide you home. In fact, you can always return to eat from them whenever you get lost in life."

While it did not make sense in my mind, what he said struck a chord in my heart. I loved to climb and I trusted what he was saying. There was something about him that made me want to listen to his every word. He looked at me with such wonder in his eyes, as if he was about to reveal an ancient treasure chest.

"Did you know, Tom, that these eight trees were planted and started growing when you were born?"

"Really?" I responded shyly, feeling embarrassed that the trees could be about me.

"These trees have been growing with you and will continue to do so for as long as you are climbing them throughout your life. When you are young, it is easy for you to climb, but as you grow older they will grow out of reach if you continually neglect them – especially this big one in the middle."

He patted the trunk of the big tree again with the palm of his wrinkled hand. This time I looked carefully at the tree to notice that its branches spanned wide and overlapped the branches of the seven others. It looked like it was supporting them.

"What is so special about this big tree?" I asked.

"This tree is your Tree of Health, Tom." He stopped to look at me and smiled as if he was introducing me to a long-lost brother or sister.

"You need to spend your life climbing this tree along with the seven others that surround it. The Tree of Love, the Tree of Family, the Tree of Work, the Tree of Friendship, the Tree of Learning, the Tree of Wealth and the Tree of Charity."

He listed and pointed to each one like a father would name his children.

"These are your eight Trees of Life, Tom. There is great wisdom in them. You will find that when you climb each one daily, you will experience completeness. And you will achieve happiness and success in ways you would never have imagined."

I was now convinced that I was in a dream. What the old man was saying sounded too fantastic. But I also believed in all things magical, so I started to accept what he was telling me. Dream or not, it sounded too intriguing to run from. I was being introduced to *my* Trees of Life and I wanted to know more about them.

A Higher Branch

CHAPTER 2

The Wise Old Man

"An old man is twice a child."

William Shakespeare

The morning sun inched higher in the sky and the old man invited me to sit with him below the big tree in the middle, the one he called the Tree of Health.

"I want to tell you a story, Tom. A story about my life. Would you like to hear it?"

"Yes," I replied hesitantly, not knowing how long his story would take. I wanted to get on with finding my way home, but was interested to hear about the old man's life. His mysterious appearance sparked my curiosity. Maybe he lived a life of adventure that would give me fodder for tales I could tell my family and friends back home.

"I will share my story with you," he said, "but you must promise me two things."

"What's that, sir?"

"First, you must pay very careful attention, so that you never forget what I tell you. Second, that you share this story with your family, friends, and everyone you meet on your life's journey."

I did love to tell stories but was intrigued as to why the old man insisted I do so. Maybe he wanted other people to know about his life.

"I will," I replied. "But why is this story so important?"

"Stories are as old as mankind itself, Tom. And our life's tale only has meaning when it is shared with others. That is how one generation teaches the next. That is why you too must share this story with everyone you care about."

The old man shifted to get comfortable. He looked rather happy to be sharing his story with me.

"In life we all go through a number of stages that present us with different challenges. These sometimes distract us from climbing and eating the fruit from all of these eight wonderful trees.

"I have been through all these stages in my life, and looking back now, I see the mistakes I made, and more importantly, the lessons I have learned."

He paused for a minute to regain his breath. He took what looked like a small bottle of medicine out of his pocket and sipped from it. I wanted to ask what it was for, but he continued before I could build up the courage.

"These eight Trees revealed to me the most powerful wisdom of all," he whispered, as if he was sharing the most magical secret in the world. "What I am about to share with you, Tom, will bring amazing success into your life. The type of success that most adults only dream about, and never get to experience.

"When I was a young boy about your age, I loved to climb trees just like you," he said with a twinkle in his eyes. "I remember waking early every morning as soon as I heard the birds come to life in the trees outside. I would rush to the window to greet the sun and the promise of a brand-new day. From that early morning rise to the moment I went to sleep, I saw life as one big adventure waiting to unfold. It was almost effortless for me to climb each Tree of my life.

"In the Tree of Health, I played lots of sports that kept me fit and energetic. And, I was well nourished because I usually ate a home-cooked meal.

"I spent a lot of time in the Tree of Family. My family and I ate dinner together almost every night. On weekends we all helped to prepare the evening meal and took turns in washing up. Most nights we spent our time reading or playing games. We rarely watched television. We talked and listened to each other's thoughts and feelings.

"I also spent a lot of time in the Tree of Friendship. My friends and I spent time together at school. We also took turns visiting each other's homes. But most of the time we played ball games in the park."

As he spoke, I looked up at the eight Trees and realised that the old man was telling me how he spent time in each of them, during what he called his 'wonder years'.

"I even climbed the Tree of Love," he said. "My parents bought me a puppy when I was eight. I would feed him, brush his coat and take him for long walks every day. He also sat next to me when I did my homework. I loved my little brown furry friend."

I caught a glimpse of the old man's eyes as they shone brilliantly in the sun. When he spoke about his dog I imagined him as a little boy just like me. I began to feel a connection with him and wanted to know more about his life.

"I also learned to climb the Tree of Work and the Tree of Wealth when I was only a young boy," he continued. "I learned that to buy the things I wanted, I would have to save for them. So I decided to earn money by doing chores around the house. I also did chores for people in my neighbourhood. When I was twelve years old, my parents allowed me to work in the local hardware store sweeping the floor and unpacking boxes. At first, I bought lots of candy with the money I earned. But eventually, I learned that if I saved enough, I could buy more important things like my first bicycle."

I interrupted and said, "When I am in high school, I want to get a real job and earn my own money. I want to be able to buy my own things. I want to surprise mum and dad. Maybe when I earn enough, I can buy them a gift."

The old man looked at me like a proud father would and said, "You are a charitable boy, Tom. Climbing the Tree of Charity does indeed begin at home but I hope you also extend this generous nature to others.

"When I was young, I climbed the Tree of Charity by giving my time to a special cause. At school they made us aware of the starving children in Africa. They inspired us to help raise money by going around the neighbourhood asking for donations. The money was to be used to buy food for children just like me.

"I was a shy child, Tom, but my passion for raising money for people less fortunate than I gave me the courage to go from door to door, asking for donations. I loved the feeling of making a difference, and my neighbours liked seeing a young boy like me doing something for the world. I think it gave them hope for the future."

He paused to reflect. It looked like he was imagining himself as a boy.

"If only all adults were as brave as that little boy," he said. "If only all adults knew what it would be like to humble themselves to a cause greater than their own. If only I had stayed as brave as that little boy for the rest of my life."

"Why do you talk about yourself as if you were another boy?" I asked.

He smiled and replied, "I now look back on my youth knowing that they were the best years of my life. You cannot imagine how life changes as you get older, Tom, but it does. And much of it will be outside of your control.

"I am of course the same person I was as a little boy, but I lost my courage and fearlessness on my way to adulthood. Worse than that, I lost my own Garden of Happiness. I forgot to climb the most important Trees in my life."

"Did you get lost like I am now?"

"Yes, Tom, but in a different way. You will most certainly find your way home much faster than I did. I lost myself, not in a meadow as pretty and sunny as this. I lost myself in the dark woods where there was no light. I lost my energy and I lost my dreams. I grew so weak in body and mind that I could not climb my own Trees of Life."

The old man paused to look down as if he was reflecting on some bad old memories. Silence filled the air. He finally looked at me, smiled and said, "Come with me, Tom. I want to show you something."

He stood up and started walking. I followed diligently. We left the shade of the eight Trees until we were in the open sun, standing on the lush green grass of the meadow. I looked back at the circle of trees, then to the old man for a cue.

"There is something you must know about these Trees," he said in a serious voice. "When you neglect them, they will stop producing fruit on the lower lying branches. And the fruit on the higher branches will become difficult for you to reach. That is why you must keep climbing them daily throughout your life. It takes courage but it is never without reward."

I knew that he was right. I always felt great when I reached for a branch to climb higher. Maybe that applied in life, too. I thought I was beginning to understand what he was telling me.

As I contemplated climbing, I saw the morning sun rising a little higher in the sky, peaking over the furthest hill in the distance. I looked up and started recounting each tree in the circle. There was something about them that seemed as wise as the old man. If only they could talk, I thought. I imagined they would have many stories to tell.

The old man's life and the eight Trees intrigued me. I was not ready to go in search of home just yet.

CHAPTER 3

Tree of Learning

*"The only thing that interferes with
my learning is my education."*

Albert Einstein

The Student Years

As we walked around the circle of the eight Trees, the old man suddenly stopped and looked up at the sun. He closed his eyes and smiled as if he was bathing his face with warmth and happiness. He looked down at me with that same smile and asked me to follow him back under the branches of one of the trees.

We found a spot near the trunk of one that had intricate lines all over it. We sat down and settled into a cross-legged position. He looked like he was preparing to tell me a long story.

"Life begins to change dramatically when we start going to school," he said. "From the moment we set foot in primary school, we surrender ourselves. We surrender our freedom and our creativity. And as we grow into our early teens we are told by our parents and teachers to 'get serious'. We are ordered to get our head out of the clouds and into our books. We are told that to obtain a good job we must focus on learning and achieving good grades. And learn we do. We learn to stop moving and to sit still for hours in a classroom full of students told to do the same.

"I remember this period in my life all too well, Tom. My mind became preoccupied with schoolwork. I stopped smiling as much. I would fidget in my chair in class and my mind would wander to other things I would rather be doing. I missed spending time alone in my room, just sitting and daydreaming. And I missed going for spontaneous wanderings into the woods.

"I do not remember when it was that I stopped climbing trees. It must have been somewhere between my daydreams and my new school timetable. It was like having something stolen from me without me even realising."

It was as if the old man was describing *my* life at school. I wondered how it was possible that, despite the many years between us, his recollections so accurately expressed the way I felt. I too hated sitting for long periods in class. I too fidgeted. I too was told to focus on getting good grades. I was told to behave as an adult, but I knew that I was still just a child and I was treated like one.

I did not like the feeling of having to stick to the routine of school that was set by the clock on the wall and our noisy school bell. I didn't like being told when to eat, when to play and when to sit down. When I was at home I could be myself, but when I was at school, I felt like my time and daydreams were taken from me. I felt like a bird whose wings had been clipped.

As my mind reflected back to the dreary hallway of the school building, the old man continued. "When I was in high school, I began to spend less and less time in the Tree of Family. Regular evening meals with my family seemed a distant memory. And spending time together reading and playing games was virtually gone. I also stopped spending time with my pet dog. Sometimes, I would pass him and not even acknowledge his playful begs for attention. My parents started complaining that I didn't feed or walk him, but how could I? I was so busy, thinking about all the homework I had to do.

"Sure I did have my friends, and as we grew older and into senior school, we spent a lot of time together. We talked about homework, our marks, what university we hoped to get into and ultimately what job we would aim for. But we never talked about our talents and our passions. We never talked about the jobs we were suited for, or the contribution we would make to society. Instead, we focused on which jobs would pay the most money. We were made to believe that making money would make us happy.

"We were never taught to embrace learning or that learning was a lifelong journey. Rather, we were made to feel like it was a temporary obligation in our younger years to prepare us for work.

"Don't get me wrong, Tom. Going to school was certainly fun at times. But it was also a place where I lived more and more inside my head. By the time I arrived at university, almost all of my time was spent sitting and working at my desk."

The old man paused and lowered his head slightly.

"My dog died whilst I was at university. My mother telephoned to tell me while I was on my way to the next lecture. After I hung up, I said to my friend, 'My dog just died,' like it was no big deal, and then went about the rest of my day. Later that night, I woke up and recalled a flood of memories of my puppy and I playing together. I remembered his whimpers for attention on the first few nights when he came to live with us. I remembered playing rumbles with him in the backyard and

how he would always come to lick my face if I accidentally hurt
him, as if to say 'its okay, I still love you'. I remembered how he
loved to play tug of war with an old shoe and how he would tilt
his head to look at me whenever I walked away with it. Most
of all, I remembered how he would always be waiting for me
at the front gate when I arrived home from school.

"I started to cry as I remembered all these fond memories.
A part of me also cried because of the regret I felt for neglecting
him in my teen years. I cried into my pillow so my roommate
could not hear. I sobbed like a little boy. I miss that little boy."

I sat, totally absorbed by his story. I imagined how terrible it
would be for me to start neglecting my own dog, Woody.

The old man took a deep breath and continued, "During my
years in high school and university, I did not participate in many
sports. Climbing the Tree of Health became a chore. I stopped
eating healthy food from home and started eating fast food and
drinking lots of sugary drinks to get me through the day.

"I now think back on when I was a boy and how climbing
trees kept my body strong and energetic. That effortless and
fun way of exercising was replaced by a regimented form of
exercise set by my school.

"If I could have chosen any sport to do at school, it would
have been gymnastics. I suppose my days of climbing trees
toned my muscles for the sport. But nobody ever saw that
potential in me, and no one ever suggested it to me, not even
my parents. So I kept that interest in gymnastics to myself, a
talent hidden from the rest of the world. I have often wondered
how my life would have turned out if I had pursued that sport.
I think I would have been much happier and no doubt healthier.
What new friends would I have made? What achievements
could I have fulfilled? Could I have made it to the Olympics
and represented my country? I will never know the answer to
any of these questions, and isn't that a horrible regret to have?"

"Why didn't you just tell someone?" I burst out in frustration.

"I was so busy doing so much homework that I spent less and less time at home communicating with my parents. We never had the chance to talk in depth about the possibility of pursuing gymnastics. So I never realised that it was an option. And, it never occurred to me to ask. I needed somebody to guide me to it, because the love I had for gymnastics was not a burning flame of passion. It was just a little spark. It needed someone to fan it to see if it burned brightly."

The old man began to get a little fired-up.

"I often felt embarrassed to speak up about my talents at school. We were certainly not encouraged to talk about anything other than the core subjects. I didn't know that school could be a place to discover anything other than what was in our textbooks. We were only ever graded on the subjects we studied, and if we didn't do well, we simply had to try harder. We weren't ever allowed to stop doing a subject if we were not passionate about it, or if we were not good at it. The teacher's focus was on improving our weaknesses rather than finding and magnifying our strengths."

Learning to Discover Your Talents

"It frustrates me to think of the many bright young people out there who have a hidden talent and a passion that is yet to be discovered. What an injustice to their families who never get to see that talent. What a tragedy for humankind if we never get to experience their greatness!

"Think of the great people who have ever lived, Tom. There is not that many when you consider the billions who have walked the earth over the centuries. Think of the contribution these people have made to the human race in the areas of law, medicine, art, literature, music, science, commerce, design, engineering and exploration. Now imagine if everyone who ever walks this Earth now and in the future could discover the talent that they were born with. Imagine the discoveries. Imagine the inventions. Imagine the progress. Imagine the richness of culture and creativity of design. Imagine the happiness that would spread on this planet if everyone lived with a passionate purpose in life!"

Hearing the old man talk like this got me excited about my own potential. Maybe I too had a hidden talent yet to be discovered.

"How do I discover *my* talent?" I asked.

"It's simple, Tom," he replied. "You must climb the seven branches on this Tree of Learning," he pointed upwards.

I looked up, a little baffled, and counted seven branches. I wondered what each branch could represent. Were they subjects at school?

"I can see that you are associating learning with school," he wisely understood. "I'm not only referring to school. That is merely one avenue of learning. At school we are mainly taught things that are *external* to us. Therefore we never develop self-awareness. And when we do not have self-awareness, it is very difficult for us to discover our talent and our inner genius."

"What is self-awareness?" I asked.

"It is an *internal* adventure, Tom. It is where we learn about all aspects of ourselves – especially our thoughts and feelings. Only when we know ourselves can we know our talents."

"So, how do I learn about myself?"

"Just look up. You will find the answer to any of life's questions in these Trees. To learn about yourself, you must learn to climb your Tree of Health, Tree of Love, Tree of Family, Tree of Friendship, Tree of Work, Tree of Wealth and Tree of Charity. They represent the seven branches on the Tree of Learning. *That* is what you should be learning throughout your life. Only then can you discover the beauty inside your heart and mind.

Only then can you find the hidden genius that lies within you.

"When you consciously and consistently learn about these areas of your life, you will start to develop a sense of who you really are and what you really want. You will start to discover your talents through that self-awareness. When you start to learn as a part of self-discovery and not obligation, you learn with intuition. You learn through creativity. When you are given the freedom to learn what you want, you start to act with responsibility and purpose. Learning becomes a part of who you are for life, and not just an obligation during your younger years. You become inquisitive and curious. Your talents and inner genius will then present itself in a magical way."

"But what if I do not have genius?" I asked.

"We all have a talent that has potential for genius, Tom. Every human is born with a talent that is different to anyone else because no two humans are born the same. We are all different. We don't look the same and we certainly do not think or feel the same. So we must all have a talent that can be applied in a unique way. How and where we apply that talent is what leads to genius. When you build self-awareness in each of these Trees, you give yourself the opportunity to discover the how and where."

The old man became animated. He jumped to his feet, pointed to each of the trees and said, "If I was in charge of all education on this Earth, I would make sure that everyone learned how to climb each of their own Trees of Life. And most of all, I would make sure that every parent and teacher was responsible for guiding every child to discover their inner genius. If you remember anything from me today, Tom, this lesson is certainly one of the most important.

"From the moment we become old enough to understand about life, we must start learning about each of these areas. For you, Tom, that time is now.

"In the Tree of Health you must learn about what to eat and what is most nutritious for your body. You must learn about the exercise routines that are best suited for you. And you must learn how to relax. In some cultures, children are taught the art of relaxation from a very young age.

"In the Tree of Love you must learn to be a thoughtful and affectionate partner.

"In the Tree of Family you must learn how to be a caring and supportive family member. You must learn to really listen and pay attention to your family's thoughts and feelings.

"In the Tree of Work you must learn how to perform to your best ability. You must also learn to be genuine in the service of others.

"In the Tree of Friendship you must learn how to make and nurture real and lasting friendships.

"In the Tree of Wealth you must learn about investing in yourself and saving your money so you can enjoy freedom in your older years.

"In the Tree of Charity you must learn about the plight of others who are less fortunate than you. You cannot just shut out the suffering of other humans on this planet by pretending they do not exist, Tom. We are all connected and it is our obligation to learn about them, so to better understand how to help."

He paused briefly, faced me and added, "These areas of your life are not learned by accident, Tom. They need to be studied just as you would any school subject."

"But how do I learn about these areas of my life if they do not teach them at school?" I asked.

"You have to go searching for knowledge yourself," he replied. "There are many books written by caring people who have taken the time to educate us about health, love, family, work, friendship, wealth and charity. You just have to go looking for these books in libraries and bookstores."

Curiosity

"I have to also warn you, Tom, that there is so much information out there that it may get a bit confusing. You must learn to take from books what is relevant to you because what works for someone else may not work for you. There is however one teacher you can always rely on to guide you in your journey as you climb the Tree of Learning. Do you know who that teacher is?"

"No," I replied, thinking that it must be someone great who has written many books.

"Your own curiosity!" he exclaimed. "Curiosity is your best teacher, Tom. Never forget that. Take responsibility for your own learning. Never rely solely on others, including your school teachers. They can guide you to knowledge but they cannot teach you self-awareness. Only one thing teaches that and that is your own curiosity. You must apply your curiosity when reading books. That means really thinking about what is stated in books and how it may apply in your life. Be that curious person that questions everything before accepting it."

He paused again, before adding, "There is also another area of knowledge, apart from books, where you can apply your curiosity.

"People," he revealed thoughtfully. "There is vast knowledge to be gained from listening to others. You must master the skill of listening. You can learn so much from other people when you listen to them with undivided attention. Learning by listening is a very fast way of acquiring knowledge. You can never know everything in life but by listening to others you can learn from their experience and that accelerates your learning.

"Listening is a dying art. Many people overindulge in constant talking that they go through life never really learning from others."

The old man laughed and added, "You know, Tom, we have

two ears and only one mouth. When it comes to learning we must listen twice as much as we talk."

*W*hat the old man taught me about the Tree of Learning left a deep impression on me throughout my years as a student. It empowered me to look at school objectively, only applying the lessons that were relevant.

Just as the old man predicted, school made me think that learning was all about attaining good grades and getting a good job. I was never taught what I wanted to learn, but what the curriculum outlined. Had I been given the freedom to choose my learning, I would have embraced it. Instead, I expressed my defiance by doing the bare minimum in subjects I had no talent for or interest in.

I took the old man's advice and taught myself about all areas of life. I studied books on health, love, family, work, friendship, wealth and charity. There were not that many at the time, but the ones I did find were insightful books by pioneering minds.

After many years of private learning I began to discover my own ideas on how to live and express my talents. It was through these ideas that I developed self-awareness. They led me to many opportunities that I seized. What I learned privately became the real reason for my achievements, personally and professionally. Learning to climb to a higher branch in all eight Trees taught me to be a healthier person, a loving partner, a supportive father, a caring brother, a fun friend, an inspirational leader, a visionary entrepreneur and an empathetic, charitable member of society.

CHAPTER 4

Tree of Love

"Stand together yet not too near together:
For the pillars of the temple stand apart,
And the oak tree and the cypress grow
not in each other's shadow."

Kahlil Gibran

I was too young to know much about love; at least that's what
I thought. The old man had a way of relating that helped me
understand what it meant to love another with all your heart
and mind. The lessons he taught me had a profound impact
on my relationships, which without a doubt became one of the
most rewarding aspects of my life.

He taught me that to love another deeply, I must first
love myself. He taught me about the Braided Branch on the
Tree of Love.

After he finished talking to me about the Tree of Learning, the old man asked me to walk with him to the next tree in the circle. He sat on the ground at the base of the tree and leaned back on the trunk. I sat opposite him and prepared to listen. He started speaking with a broad smile on his face, like he was imagining himself as a young man again.

"When I was twenty-one years old I met my first serious girlfriend, Sarah," he said. "It was during this time of my life that I spent a lot of time in the Tree of Love.

"The Tree of Love is amazing, Tom. It holds the most delicious fruit in our Garden of Happiness although it does not have much fruit on its branches. Sometimes, when you think you see the fruit, the winds of change will blow and you will lose sight of it. So when you do eventually find it, you must sit and savour it. You should not rush, because the fruit from the Tree of Love is so hard to find and so easy to lose.

"My early days with Sarah were filled with much excitement. She was the first thing on my mind when I woke up and the last thing I thought about before nodding off to sleep. I was so excited about my love for her that I wanted to share it with the world.

"I understand that you are a young boy and cannot comprehend the feeling of adult love just yet, but I have no doubt that one day you will experience this wonderful feeling."

I looked down shyly.

He chuckled and said, "I can see you may be a little embarrassed about this topic, Tom."

I was curious about love because I had seen my mother and father kiss and cuddle at home. So I really did want to know more.

"At the beginning of a relationship, it is very easy to love," he continued. "You are finding out new and exciting things about the other person. You also start to see the wonderful qualities that person brings out in you. You become a warm and friendly person with a caring attitude. And people will notice your positive outlook on life.

"You will feel like your future is full of unlimited potential. You will dream of travelling together to all parts of the world and experiencing different cultures, meeting new people, seeing great sights and trying new foods. You will also start to dream about the future you will both create together. That is what love does to you. It makes you dream about your future. And the very best part is that you have someone to share it with."

The old man paused, sighed and added, "I miss my Sarah. I miss the love we had."

"Why? What happened?" I asked.

"Well, Tom, sometimes a relationship goes bad and people fall out of love with one another. Or they think they do, because they stop climbing to a higher branch in their Tree of Love."

He looked down as if hanging his head in shame and said, "At one point, later in life, Sarah and I parted ways."

I paused to think about my next question for fear that it may be too personal, but my curiosity got the better of me. "If being in love makes you feel so good, why did you and Sarah part?"

"I wish I could answer that question easily, Tom, but I can't. The only thing I can explain is the mistakes I made in the relationship and what I have learned.

Two Ways Love Goes Wrong

"I made two mistakes when it came to the Tree of Love. I spent too much time on it when I first met Sarah and I did not spend enough time on it after we got married and had a family of our own.

"You see, Tom, there is something very important you need to know about the Tree of Love."

He picked up a stick and started to draw a love heart on the ground. He drew a line down the middle so it was split into two. He then said with some precision, "The Tree of love is the most vulnerable of the eight Trees in your Garden of Happiness. You need to spend just the right amount of time on it. If you do not spend enough time, you will neglect it and if you spend too much time, you will spoil it."

The old man placed the stick on the side of the trunk and asked me, "Do you like music?"

"Yes. I listen to music when I am alone in my room," I replied.

"Well, love is a lot like music. It is deep with meaning and rich with layers of instrumental arrangement. It must be listened to attentively with focus and no distraction. And it can only be enjoyed and appreciated when your own life is lived with similar layers of richness and meaning. Otherwise, you will hear the music of love but not truly know it in your heart."

The old man seemed to talk in a reflective tone that was as much for his ears as it was for mine.

"How do I have a rich and meaningful life?" I asked.

"By living a complete life in these eight Trees," he promptly responded. "Climbing higher in these Trees gives us meaning and richness. We become interesting people with knowledge, experience, empathy, creativity and passion. Climbing these Trees takes us on a journey that develops all these qualities in us. And when we have these qualities, we learn to identify love, appreciate love, and really know love. And when you really know love, you begin to show it and express it. You become a loving partner. You become thoughtful with your words and with your actions."

I smiled at the thought of my mother and father being affectionate. My sister Sophia and I often walked in on them hugging in the kitchen.

"But you should not listen to a beautiful song too many

times, Tom," the old man advised. "Otherwise you will grow too familiar with it. Perhaps even tired of it. Likewise with this Tree of Love, you cannot spend too much time on it. Otherwise you will exhaust its fruit too quickly."

Spoiling Love

"The big lesson that I have learned from my early days with Sarah is that if you spend too much time on the Tree of Love, you can actually spoil the love itself," he said poignantly. "And do you know why this happens? Because early in the relationship, you can neglect the other areas of your life. You focus too much on your partner and forget about your health, family, friendships, learning, work, wealth and charity. You start looking for your Garden of Happiness in that solitary Tree of Love.

"You begin to attach your internal happiness to the person you love and you become dependent on them. When that happens, you can lose yourself along the way. And when you lose yourself, there is nothing left for the other person to love. And there is nothing about yourself that you will love either."

He paused and added, "If there is one thing I have learned, Tom, it is this. Loving another person comes from the same part of your heart as loving yourself," he pointed to the heart that he drew on the ground.

He turned from the trunk and lowered himself all the way back to lie on the ground. He lay there gazing up at the tree, as if he was witnessing something truly spectacular, "Look up, Tom, and notice how one branch of love is like a braid of two smaller branches."

I too laid back on the ground and gazed up. I tried to fix my eyes on the sunshine peeking through the leaves, but as I focused on what he said, I noticed the most beautiful branch that I had ever seen. It was made up of two small branches wrapped around each other in a spiral up towards the sun.

They were as perfectly braided as my sister's hair on a Sunday morning.

I turned to the old man in amazement.

"It's beautiful, isn't it, Tom?" he said with a broad smile.

"It looks amazing," I replied. "How can a branch be made up of two smaller ones? How is that possible?"

"Each little branch represents love," he answered. "One branch is the love you have for yourself and the other is the love you have for your sweetheart. They both support and nourish each other beautifully. They both bear fruit like no other. But know this," he cautioned in a somber voice, "if one branch dies, the other one dies as well. That is both the splendour and the tragedy of this Braided Branch."

I felt my heart swell up with wonder.

Loving yourself

"I want this Braided Branch to be your reminder that the secret to loving another is to always love yourself," he said.

"I don't understand. How do I love myself?"

"By living a complete life in these eight Trees of Life and by not neglecting any."

"How will that help me to love myself?"

"To love yourself, Tom, you must have your own goals and dreams in each of these eight Trees and not just the Tree of Love. You must continue to live your life completely while you are in love. You must give yourself time and space to do that. I spoiled my love for Sarah because early on in the relationship, I stopped focusing on the other areas of my life, especially my family and friends, and my career."

"Did you spend too much time with Sarah?" I asked.

"Yes Tom. We suffocated our love. We exhausted the fruit too quickly. We stopped being the people we were before we met; the very person that the other fell in love with. We stopped being fun, spontaneous, curious and ambitious. As for me, I spent less time with my family and even less time with friends. I ceased my learning and lost focus on what I really wanted to do in my career. Nothing else seemed to matter at the time. That was fine for a little while, but when we ran out of fruit we started to feel a little stale, like something was missing. We started to worry that maybe something was wrong with our relationship."

I started to worry whether that could ever happen to my mum and dad.

"So what should you do when that happens?" I asked.

"To nurture a loving relationship, you must spend time nurturing yourself. Chase your own dreams. Spend time alone in reflection. Spend time with your family. Cultivate your own friendships. Play a sport. Look and feel your best. Learn something you are passionate about. Pursue your ambitions. Create your own wealth. And give yourself to charity. Your partner will love you even more for it. You will become an interesting person to talk to and be with. And your love will grow stronger."

Neglecting Love

It occurred to me that although the old man made some mistakes early on in his relationship, he and Sarah still stayed together, because he mentioned that they had a family.

"But you and Sarah were married for so many years?" I asked.

"Well, Tom, when you spend too much time on this branch, it will spoil but not die. You can always revive it. But when you *neglect* it for a long time, it will most definitely die. And that's what eventually happened to our love.

"Even though we spoiled it early in the relationship, Sarah and I were still committed to staying together because we cared deeply for each other. We couldn't figure out at the time why our love felt flat but we still managed our way through it. There were happy times. It just wasn't the kind of happiness that we could have achieved had we both lived a complete life. It was mediocre. Not brilliant, but not bad either.

"It was during this period in our relationship that we both turned our back on the Tree of Love and started neglecting it; because we no longer found happiness in it. We went from spending too much time together to not spending enough time. We started to focus on other areas of our life, especially work.

"But here is the thing about this branch, Tom. You must constantly return to it for nourishment, otherwise the fruit just sits there waiting for you. Over time the fruit will ripen and fall from the tree uneaten – wasted. You may get away with ignoring it for a while, but when it is repeatedly left uneaten, you will find that the branch will stop producing any fruit at all. That's what happened to Sarah and I. Our fruit on the Tree of Love dried up and we could not nourish our love anymore. Our love withered along with the Braided Branch on each of our Trees of Love. And worse still, we started to blame each other for it. By the time we had figured it out, it was too late. There was no more fruit left to bring our love back to life."

The old man appeared sad.

"Great love does not just happen by accident, Tom. It needs attention and regular nourishment. If I could go back and do it all again, I would have been a more thoughtful partner. I would have given Sarah daily hugs and kisses. I would have held her hand whenever we walked in public. I would have told her daily about all her wonderful qualities. And I would have written little notes to remind her.

"There are so many ways that I can now think of to have expressed my love. I now realise that all it required was for me to love Sarah just as much as I should have loved myself."

He got up off the ground and stood looking up at the Tree of Love in reflection. I too stood and looked up waiting to learn more from him about life.

My personal experience has proven that loving yourself is difficult and loving another even more so. But I have learned that nothing good in life comes easy, including love. You have to work hard at it by focusing just as relentlessly on love as you would on your career and on your wealth. You have to pursue love with the same passion and intensity as you would any other goal. Why? Because love completes and defines us.

There are some who feel that they do not need love and intimacy in their life. That may be okay for a time, but I have learned that expressing love awakens a power and energy so strong that it lifts your level of performance in all areas of life to that of extraordinary. It connects the power of your mind with that of your heart and unleashes a source of immense creativity and imagination. Many a brilliant song or artwork or literature or some architectural feat has been created by someone in love. It is a tragedy to let such a source of great power be left to chance or, even worse, wasted.

CHAPTER 5

Tree of Family

*"In family life,
be completely present."*

Lao Tzu

*B*eing completely present at home has been one of my biggest challenges in life. Although the wise old man taught me many lessons about the importance of family, I struggled for many years to focus on this Tree of Life without distraction. I guess that sometimes it is only through personal experience that we learn to appreciate the fruit from this tree, that so many of us take for granted.

Often it is when we meet with failure and face obstacles in life that we are prompted to seek the support of our family. That's when we truly appreciate the unconditional love that our family has for us – a love that is greater than any.

The old man began to tire a little after he finished talking about the Tree of Love. The stories he shared seemed to drain his energy. I wondered if it was because it made him sad to remember the love he neglected.

He asked me to walk with him to the next tree in the circle. When we arrived at the bottom of the tree he asked me to remain standing.

"This is the tree I also like to call the tree of support," he said as he patted the solid trunk. "It is where family grow together and support each other. It is your Tree of Family, Tom," he looked and smiled at me.

"This is the Tree that I took for granted. Along with Health and Love, this is the Tree I most neglected in my life and the reason why I lost my way."

I knew that sometimes I also took my family for granted. My father and mother worked very hard to make our family life a happy one. They set rules that I questioned regularly. Rules like eating together rather than in front of the television and other rules like tidying my room. At that moment, I felt guilty for disobeying them. I wondered if that was the reason I got lost in the meadow. Suddenly I felt a pang of sadness in my heart.

"This is the Tree that protects your heart, Tom," the old man continued, as if he read my mind. "The heart that carries your love for others and the heart that dares to dream big goals in life."

As he spoke, I looked up at the tree and noticed that there were three branches on my Tree of Family. The old man explained that the number of branches is different for everyone because each branch represented a family member. There was one for my father, one for my mother and one for my sister Sophia. He said that many more branches would grow when I had a family of my own. He also explained that each branch would support and protect me for as long as I was climbing it. This meant spending time with each member of my family, showing them love and support. It also meant listening to them with undivided attention.

He pointed at the three branches and said, "You will notice, that this tree also supports a branch that reaches from the Tree of Love – the branch of unconditional love; the love that you have for your family, Tom."

I looked up again to notice that the Tree of Family cradled the branch of unconditional love. It resembled a baby being held in its mother's arms.

"This Tree protects your heart because it is the Tree that helps you manage all the setbacks that life may bring you. Life is not perfect, and we too are not perfect. Things will happen outside of our control, even when we do our best. So we will sometimes experience sadness and pain, whether it is from illness, failure, rejection, conflict, heartbreak or disappointment. But do you know who to turn to when life deals you such blows?"

"My family," I answered.

I knew exactly what the old man meant by unconditional love. My mother often said seven words to me that were the cradle of support for my heart. She would say them whenever I came home from school with hurt feelings; either from doing poorly in an exam or failing to make the soccer team. Whatever the disappointment, my mother only ever had to say these seven words to lift my spirits and make me feel valued. She would say, 'I love you always, no matter what.'

This was Mum's way of saying that no matter what I did and no matter what happened, she would always love me and have a special place in her heart for me. It made me feel like I could take on any challenge without fear, because I knew that I had her support regardless of whether I succeeded or failed.

Yes, I certainly knew the importance of family because my parents supported my whole existence. I wondered how such a wise old man could fail on this important Tree of Life. It made me curious to learn what mistakes he made. Was there something I did not know about family? Was there a mistake that I might also make when I was older?

So I asked him, "But you are so wise, how could you neglect your own family? I could never imagine doing that."

He replied in a humble voice, "I love your honesty, Tom. I wish I had your wisdom when I was a family man.

"Let me tell you about the next stage of my life that confused my priorities."

The Marriage Years

"Sarah and I loved each other so much that we decided to get married. It was the next natural step in our relationship and a way of keeping the excitement alive. We couldn't wait to live together and find a place of our own to call home.

"We started spending most of our time talking about saving money to buy an apartment. It was exciting at first to be preparing for the wedding and buying things for our new home, but it was during this period that we also forgot about the simple pleasures.

"When we eventually got married and moved into our apartment, matters only got worse. We worked such long hours and arrived home so late that Sarah and I spent less and less time enjoying each other's company. We were so tired that we would just flop in front of the television and not talk much. We had spent most of our energy talking all day at work.

"The only thing that seemed to give us joy was going shopping on weekends to buy things for ourselves. We didn't see our parents and friends as often and visited even less. We did manage to keep exercising a little. We made a pact to go for walks together in the morning and again after work. But when the winter weather began to bite, we were not as disciplined."

The old man's story sounded like it did not have a happy ending.

"Sarah and I continued to work very hard in our jobs. We both achieved job promotions and started spending a lot of time at work. We seemed to be thriving on accomplishing our career goals and making money. We were not happy during this time, but we were not sad either.

"You know, Tom, when most couples get married they are not given a practical guide to family life. They have to try and figure it out for themselves. Unfortunately, Sarah and I did not make the effort to work on our relationship like we did on our careers. We never brought our awareness to it. We assumed that a happy marriage was something that just happened effortlessly. When in truth it needed to be learned and worked on just as much as our careers."

The Parenting Years

"Sarah and I loved each other but as the days went by we did not show it as much. There was something missing in our relationship but we could not figure out what it was. It was then that we talked about having children. We thought that having a child would bring us closer together and give us a purpose. Two years later Sarah gave birth to our beautiful baby girl, Penny.

"Sarah stopped working after we had Penny. I was making enough money for her to give up her job and stay home. Both Sarah and I loved Penny so much that we spent most of our time and energy on her – especially Sarah. This was a wonderful period in our life because we had so much love to give. I remember thinking at the time that I could never love anyone or anything as much as I loved Penny."

He paused to reflect and added, "But it was also during this period that I neglected the other areas of my life. I made no time for friends, fun or exercise."

I imagined how sad it would be if I lived my life without fun and friendship. But I was also old enough to know how parents' lives could change when they have a baby.

"It's hard work to look after babies," I said. "When my sister Sophia was born, my parents spent a lot of time with her."

"You know, Tom, it is unrealistic to think that you could devote *equal* time and attention daily to these eight Trees throughout your life. Sometimes we go through periods when we are required to spend more time on some than others. Having children is that period when we need to devote a lot of attention to the Tree of Family. But do you know what else? This focus should never be at the expense of the other areas of life *completely*. Sarah and I almost ceased socialising with our family and friends. Even less than what we did before. We also spent less time together being affectionate. We became totally absorbed by the responsibility of caring for Penny. And this, I am sure, led us down the path of an unhappy family life.

"I wish I could go back in time and relive this period of my life. I would do it differently. Instead of hibernating at home with Sarah and Penny, I would have made sure that we spent more time with family and friends. I would have used the time to exercise. I could have gone for jogs with Penny in her stroller. This would have kept me fit. I would have made sure we still went out to the park together. I would have arranged for Sarah to bring little Penny to the office so she could see where her daddy worked.

"I am sure that if we did all those things, Penny would have grown up even wiser and healthier. Children at any age know what is going on around them. They are very perceptive. If I had lived my life completely, then Penny would have had many more adventures."

"So what eventually happened?" I asked, in the hope that

things got better for him.

"Well, Tom, as Sarah settled into a routine with Penny, I gradually spent less time at home and started working longer hours. Sarah was enjoying motherhood and she developed a close bond with Penny. She also started exercising and cultivating her own friendships. I, on the other hand, exercised less and started putting on weight. I became very unfit and overweight."

"You, overweight?"

"Yes, Tom, it's hard to imagine but I was once much larger than this. Let me tell you a little story of how overweight I was. One day when Penny was five years old, she coaxed me into doing a cartwheel with her in the backyard. I thought I could, but when my hands felt the ground and tried to support my heavy body, I fell in a heap, much to the delight of Penny who giggled and giggled. She did not realise that I had injured my back when I fell. I had to go to a doctor for many months to have it mended. The sad truth was that I had allowed my fitness to deteriorate so much that I could not even play with my daughter without losing my breath and getting tired.

"Let me remind you, Tom, if you do not eat well, exercise and relax throughout your life, there will come a time when your body starts to break down. My body started giving me signs that I should have paid attention to. I had less energy. I was slower. I was fatter. And I would visit the doctor often to get medicine."

"What was the medicine for?

"For all sorts of problems. There was one to help me digest my food and another to help me sleep. To keep me functioning. But nothing worked. The pills just covered up the problem. Worst of all, I started feeling that nobody could love me the way I looked. For the first time in my life, I started feeling unhappy."

"That sounds so sad. Why didn't you just stop working so much and look after yourself?"

"I had to work harder and harder because Sarah and I borrowed lots of money from the bank to buy a big house in a fancy neighbourhood. When my health started deteriorating, I should have sold the house and moved to a smaller one in an area that we could afford; but I didn't. Things were not quite bad enough to make me want to change. I was still able to get up in the morning and go to work and drive my car and eat food. That was my version of living. I wasn't living my best life but I accepted it as a compromise and justified it by saying to myself that working such long hours was for the sake of my family. I never realised that my family would have preferred to see me healthy, energetic, and fun to be around. I fooled myself into thinking that for as long as I made enough money to buy them the things they wanted, they would be happy. The truth, Tom, is that my family became as unhappy as I was."

I knew exactly what he meant. I could never be happy when Mum or Dad or Sophia was sick. The house always seemed a bit somber when one of us was ill in bed.

I felt sorry for the old man. It must have been hard for him to live with the regret of disappointing his family. I knew how bad I felt if Mum or Dad were disappointed with me. I wondered whether he did eventually return to a happy family life.

Postponing Happiness

"What happened? Did you stop working so much to spend more time with your family?"

"Regrettably not, Tom, because I never hit rock bottom. At least when you reach your lowest point, it forces you into action. But I had not reached that point just yet. I kept telling myself that one day I would change everything. That when I paid off the mortgage I would work less, exercise more and spend more time with Sarah and Penny. But it never happened. All I was doing was delaying my happiness. It was like being lost in a deep, dark forest that kept getting darker. It got to a stage that I could not see a glimmer of light to guide me out. I acted like I had all the time in the world to change my ways. But there came a point where it was too late to reverse the course of my life. The momentum was too great."

"That must have upset your family." I said. "Penny would have missed you, I'm sure. I know I would miss my father if he spent too much time at work."

"You are right, Tom. As Penny grew older, she stopped talking to me as much. She would hide her pain by ignoring me and hanging out more and more with her friends. I lost my connection with her, as I did with my childhood sweetheart, Sarah.

"When Penny started university, she moved out of home. It was very sad to see her go and it broke my heart to notice that she was glad to be leaving our soulless home. I still remember that day clearly. She loaded her suitcases in the back of the car and turned to give me a hug goodbye. That hug was the last I received from her for many years. At that instant, all her younger years flashed before my eyes. The little girl with a ponytail and a contagious giggle was gone. It all happened so quickly that I was lost for words. I did not know what to say. How could I reverse eighteen years of poor fatherhood in a few minutes? It was all too little and too late. As the car drove off I turned to look at the front door of our home and it was then that I started to feel the emptiness. I was happy for Penny but I was sad that my only real connection with her had disappeared.

"You see, Tom, living under the same roof with your family does not give you an emotional connection with them. A bond is what makes that connection, whether they live with you or not. I felt empty because I knew I had no bond to keep Penny coming back to see me. I could tell that she was glad to be leaving and that's what broke my heart."

The old man paused and looked down. A solitary teardrop fell on his left cheek. I could tell there was much more pain behind that one tear than his eyes could muster. He wiped it with his long sleeve and looked up at me with a brave smile. Although he looked old there was something about his eyes that made him seem young at heart. They sparkled in the sunshine and appeared to contain all of the world's wisdom, as I was gradually discovering.

"I don't blame Penny for how she felt," he continued. "All those years I spent working back at the office, and sometimes on weekends, caused a permanent disconnect between us. The promises I made to her were broken so many times that this became her permanent impression of me. I became the father who promised to read to her, but never did; who promised to see her artwork when I got home, but arrived too late from work; who promised to go for a bike ride with her, but was always too tired.

"Children never forget, Tom. I don't think she ever hated me for it. She knew, and I always reminded her, that I was working hard to make money to buy her things and pay for her education. But that is not what she wanted from me. She would have preferred to have my time and attention than to have all those things that now sit collecting dust in the attic.

"Not spending enough time with Penny is one of my most painful regrets in life. I would give anything to go back in time and live a simple and modest life. I would have preferred to stay living in our first comfortable home in the neighbourhood we could afford. I would have had a small mortgage and therefore no need to work long hours. I would have spent much more time with Penny doing the things she was excited about, like reading books, riding bicycles, going to the park to kick a ball around, doing jigsaw puzzles, telling stories, playing hide and seek, and helping her with schoolwork.

"Those activities now seem so wonderfully exciting. Back then I viewed them as a chore and a distraction from real-life adult concerns of promotions, finances and client functions. I was always too preoccupied in my world to see what was going on in hers. If I could go back, I would surrender myself to that world. And I would now have the fond memories and the bond with Penny."

The old man paused momentarily in reflection.

"I have since written a poem about this regret in my life, Tom. Would you like to hear it?"

"Yes," I replied softly, sensing that the old man was sharing something personal with me.

He walked closer to the Tree of Family and reached his hand into a deep crevice inside the trunk, a place where birds would go and hide. He took out and unfolded a piece of paper that was frayed at the edges and started reading:

"Me I see.
A smile like me I see
Looking back at me
Searching for me
But do I see?
Fruit from my own tree
As bright as can be
Saying 'come play with me'
But do I see?
If I could just be
Then I would see
It was once me."

"This poem, Tom, is about how some adults forget that they were once children. When they have children of their own, it is their chance to reconnect with the wonder of childhood.

"I want you to have it," he insisted, as he folded the paper and put it in my hand.

I still have that poem.

CHAPTER 6

Tree of Work

To produce stunning fruit,
you must plant yourself in
the right field.

It was mid-morning when the old man finished talking to me about the Tree of Family. The birds were busy in the trees above us. They were squawking excitedly. It sounded like they were looking for food. It made me smile and reminded me that I was hungry.

"Are you enjoying the story, Tom?" The old man asked.

"Yes I am, but some parts are sad."

"It's okay to feel sad sometimes," he replied. "Sadness is as much a part of life as happiness. It is an expression of our compassion and shows that we can have empathy for others, which is a good thing.

"Regret is what you must be wary of. Regret feels like sadness but is so much more painful because it is something that we bring on ourselves when we focus on the past. We cannot change the past, whereas sadness can be turned into happiness by what we do now and in the future."

The old man then changed subject and said, "You must be hungry Tom. Would you like something to eat?"

"Yes please."

"Okay follow me," he said as he got up off the ground briskly. "Lets go find a spot under the tree over there," he gestured to the next tree in the circle. I remembered that it was the Tree of Work. We arrived and sat below it. He turned to face me like he had something to give. He put his hand in his pocket and took out a brown paper bag and what looked like a wrapped sandwich.

"I have a bag of figs and a peanut butter sandwich. Would you like to share these with me?"

"They are two of my favourite foods," I replied.

"They are my favourite too," he responded with a great big smile, pleased that we had something in common.

The old man was generous. He shared half of his packed lunch with me even though I was only a child.

I was so hungry that I did not talk for some time. The flavour of the figs was amazing – the best I had ever tasted. They were perfectly soft, ripe and sweet. I wanted to savour every bite.

We happily ate and looked at each other with a smile every now and then. The silence was comfortable. When we both finished he said, "I can see that you enjoyed the figs."

"Yes they are delicious, thank you."

"I bought them from a local farmer not far from here. His name is Warren. I visit his fig orchard often. He has one of the biggest orchards in the world. He has rows and rows of fig trees as far as the eyes can see.

"Wow," I replied.

"Yes, watching him work his orchard inspires me. I love to

sit and chat with him. I have learned so much about figs from him. Did you know, for example, that fig trees are very easy to plant and grow, but only if you plant them in the right field. Did you also know that fruit-eating animals prefer to eat figs to any other food, even if there is an abundance of other fruit in the woods. That must tell you something about figs."

The Wisdom of the Fig Orchard

After spending the morning with the old man, I began to realise that there was a reason for him to mention the fig orchard. So I asked him, "Why do you go to the orchard?"

"Warren is a friend of mine and I like to visit him," he answered.

"But you also said you go there to get inspired."

"You are very attentive and inquisitive, Tom. Yes there *is* another reason why I go there. Warren and his orchard of figs remind me of the wisdom on this Tree of Work.

"You will notice that there are two branches on this Tree. One is for working under the guidance of others – you will probably spend time early in your career climbing this branch. The other is when you become a person who guides others – a leader. This branch comes with great freedom and satisfaction but it also comes with great responsibility.

"I would like to share with you seven lessons about working that will help you climb both these branches and achieve greatness in your life. But before I do so, I need to tell you one very important rule. You must know and live by this rule *before* you start reaching and climbing higher in your chosen career."

Although I understood little about the adult working world, I knew that the old man's lessons on work would be important to my future. So I paid very careful attention.

Love What You Do

"You must love your work," he said. "You cannot work from the heart if you do not love what you do. Whether you work at home looking after the family or in an office with one hundred people, you must be passionate about what it is you do on a daily basis. It does not even have to be something you do for money. It can be volunteering for a cause that you care deeply about. Whatever it is, loving what you do partly defines who you are as a person.

"Work is not bad, Tom. Work is not the enemy of living. In fact, working helps you to live a great life. If you do not work, you have no purpose. Working gets you up in the morning. It fulfils you. There is nothing more rewarding at the end of the day than to feel that you have expressed your talents through your work.

"We are all born with a need to work and express our inner talent. Remember what I told you earlier at the Tree of Learning. We all have a talent that is unique to us. Well, work is a chance for us to display that talent."

The old man began to get animated as he rolled from one point to the next.

"Work is also important to our health, because loving what we do makes us feel good. And our bodies react to that in a positive way. We start to feel energised and stimulated.

"Work also helps us to relax. When we are productive at work, it makes us feel worthy of our time to relax at the end of the day, because our heart will feel contented."

He paused to reflect a little, as if he was remembering something from his working years. He lowered his voice, looked at me and said, "I know I told you earlier that I spent too much time at work, but that was not my only regret. My other regret was that I did not work for love. I worked for money.

"Loving what you do is being true to yourself, Tom. Instead,

I lied to myself and to the people I worked with. And most tellingly, I lied to the people I was supposed to serve – my customers. I did not care whether they enjoyed or valued the products we sold them. I only did it to make money and to meet budgets. I did not do it with the thought of adding value to their lives and making them happy.

"If ever you fall into the trap of working solely for money my strong advice for you is to get out quickly. This is a trap for fools – fools who chase money rather than fulfilment. You can never truly serve others and achieve success if your sole focus is money. Therefore do not ever do a job where you cannot see the connection between your work and the positive impact it has on other people's lives. Your job must add value and bring happiness to others. Otherwise, your career will never make you happy.

"I did not listen to my feelings, Tom. And after ignoring them for such a long time, I became increasingly unhappy. Work gave me the right of passage to arrive home and complain about how tired I was and how much I hated my job. I developed the attitude that I could never love it. Work became an obligation to put up with during the weekdays so I could live my real life at home on the weekends. But you know what I realised? I realised that when you do not enjoy your work, then you are never happy enough to enjoy your personal life."

The old man seemed to be annoyed with himself.

I always assumed that every adult worked in a job that they loved because they were preoccupied with asking children like me, 'What do you want to be when you grow up?' So I asked him, "What job did you really want to do?"

"I wanted to be a school teacher," he replied. "I *really* wanted to be a school teacher," he repeated.

"Really?"

"Yes Tom. That was my real talent. I had the patience and

the passion for it. And I cared very much for young minds and their future.

"I seriously thought about leaving my job. I really did. I would stay up some nights planning it and talking to Sarah about it. But I did nothing. I waited and waited for the right time, until it was too late. I became too old and by that time my family had fallen apart. Unhappiness became a way of life at home and at work. I do not remember when it was that I stopped talking about being a teacher. It all happened so slowly that my dream just faded, along with the memory of it.

"All those years I worked in the wrong job, in what I thought, was a sacrifice for my family; when really, I missed out on the most important opportunity I had as a father. My role as a father was not only to provide. It was to live my life by example. I dealt my daughter, Penny, the biggest injustice by not being a good role model. Showing courage to pursue my career as a teacher would have been the best example I could have set for her. It would have taught her the most important lesson about working. It would have taught her to never chase money at the expense of dreams.

"She did eventually learn this lesson, but it was by virtue of my cautionary tale rather than my example. She learned what *not* to do instead of what to do. It is a lesson nonetheless and I am proud of her for learning it; but it was a lesson that I'm sure was tinged with sadness. For it is much better to learn from a good example than a bad one, especially if that bad one was that of a parent you loved and once adored."

Plant Yourself in the Right Field

"I stayed in the wrong job all my life, Tom. And many of my colleagues did the same. Because we did not love our work, we needed a lot of guidance to keep us on track. The company hired experts to motivate us and teach us how to treat customers and manage our time. But they forgot one important detail. They never asked us whether we wanted to be in the job in the first place. They never asked us whether we truly loved our work. They showed no interest in our goals and dreams. If they bothered to notice what was really going on inside our hearts and minds, they would have realised that a lot of us did not belong in the company."

The old man then looked at me intently and said, "If a fig tree is planted in the wrong field, it does not matter how much fertiliser and attention you give it; it will simply not grow, flourish and produce an abundance of fruit. We are no different to the fig trees in Warren's orchard. We must plant ourselves in the right field to grow and produce good results."

"How do I know what the right field is for me?" I asked.

"It is where you can display your natural talents, Tom."

"But how will I know what my talents are?"

"You will discover them during your learning years. And once you start to apply those talents in your work of choice, you will then start to *love* what you do."

I thought I knew what the old man was getting at, but a little seed of doubt inside my mind kept me from truly believing in it. Fear of failure kicked in.

"What if I choose something and fail? Should I try something else?"

"As long as you have a *genuine* passion for your career, you should never quit!" he exclaimed passionately. "You must persist because you will eventually succeed. If you find that you are not talented at what you think you love, then it may mean that you are motivated for all the wrong reasons. Be wary of your heart's motives, Tom. You must identify whether there are negative emotions driving your heart, such as jealousy, peer pressure, wanting to impress or even the desire to please your family. If these feelings are the motivators for your pursuit, then yes, you must rethink your chosen career and try something else. You must go searching for your *true* passion instead."

"So I must pursue what I *truly* love."

"No Tom, you must *love* what you are truly good at."

"Huh? What is the difference?"

The old man smiled patiently and said, "I understand why you might be confused. Allow me to clarify. For I have learned this lesson the hard way.

"There is a big difference between doing what you love and loving what you do. The reality is that we all cannot do what we think we love. We all cannot be a rock star musician or the winner of a Nobel Peace Prize. Not all of us can be famous. When we pursue such illusive goals in our career we end up being unhappy with what we can do and what is within our ability to do right now. That is why there are so many people walking around hating their job. Because they are always thinking of what can be, instead of being happy with what is. The only thing we can control Tom, is how we feel about our job. We all can make a choice to love what we do. All I am really saying is that loving what we do comes easier and from the heart when we perform work that caters to our natural talents. Only then can we put our hand on our heart and honestly say that we are planted in the right field."

Seven Lessons on *How* to Work

The old man shifted to sit a little more upright and added, "But, once you are planted in the right field, you will need to learn how to work and grow in that field.

"I want to now share with you the seven lessons that will help you perform at your very best. If you live by these lessons when you are older, you will find amazing success in your working life."

I too sat a little more upright, my curiosity growing. I wanted to be successful when I grew up.

1. Serve people from the heart

"First and foremost, working is about serving others," he said. "Whether you work for yourself or for someone else you have to remember that you are in the humble service of people. You must work from the heart because people will feel it. They will connect with you. They will start to believe in your words and in your actions. More so, *you* will start to believe in your own work, because as humans we value ourselves in equal proportion to the value we add to others."

"What does that mean?"

"It means that we start to love our job more when we focus on serving others and making a difference in their lives.

"How do we do that?"

"We do it by working from the heart."

He paused and then added, "I have discovered that the easiest way to engage the heart is to serve others like you would your own family. It's that simple. Your work should always be held to that standard."

What the old man said reminded me of how my father worked as a builder. He was up very early most days to go to work. The sound of his truck starting was my morning alarm clock. On school holidays I often went with him to his building sites to help out. I would hear him say to his clients, 'I will treat this house like it was my own.' I liked seeing their body language shift from tense and uncertain to comfortable and enthusiastic. They would look back at my father with a trusting smile.

Yes, my father did indeed take pride in building homes for other people. 'I built another family's dream home,' he would say to me. I knew he felt good after finishing because he would be very happy at the dinner table that night. His face always had an expression of contentment. He often took a few days holiday after that. I loved those days because he would take me fishing. On those trips he would explain to me the importance of good workmanship and building something to last a lifetime. He would say, 'A lot of builders like to rush their jobs, but I don't. I want people to remember my work long after I am gone.'

My father never took on more work than he could handle, either. He said that it was greedy to do so and that he could not possibly give one hundred per cent of his effort to each project if he did.

So I understood exactly what the old man meant by serving others and working from the heart. All I had to do was picture my father's smiling face.

2. Master your craft

"This next lesson, Tom, is one that will also help you love your job more. It is one that I am very passionate about."

"Why are you passionate about it?" I interrupted.

"Because it is the essence of the wisdom of climbing higher in life. It is the simple act of daily improvement in your work. It is the constant search to better your performance and to keep learning your craft. You should never rely on your talent alone, Tom. Keep sharpening your skills. Aim to know your work inside and out. Keep practising and practising until you become an expert at your job."

"Practice makes perfect!" I said.

"Yes, Tom. Except that my idea of perfection is when you perform your job to the best of *your* ability. So, aim for progress not perfection."

"I understand what you mean, but how does that make you love your job more?" I asked.

"Quite simply because when you are good at something, you

tend to start liking it. The better you are it, the more confidence you will have in yourself and in your abilities. It's human nature to like what you are good at."

I nodded in agreement. I always liked the subjects at school that I was good at.

3. Be your best self at work

"Now, Tom. Lets get onto the third lesson. This one is very important because it will remind you to stay focused on all your other Trees of Life and not just your work. But ironically, it is one that will help you improve your work."

The old man had me intrigued. How can something that will take my focus away from work also improve it?

"Before you can be great at your work, you must be great at home," he said. "You must be the best person that you can be."

"How do I do that?" I asked eagerly. I liked the idea of being my best.

"By staying focused on these eight Trees," he replied. "These areas of your life complete you. You will not have *energy* to work if you do not eat well, exercise and relax. You will not have drive and inspiration if you do not have *love* in your life. You cannot deal with setbacks and obstacles at work if you do not have the support of your *family*. You cannot continue to improve your performance at work if you do not keep *learning*. You cannot enjoy the fun and laughter that work brings if you do not have *friends* to share it with. You will not have the freedom to continue to work for love if you do not save your money and build your *wealth*. And you cannot truly enjoy the success of your work unless you are *charitable* to others.

"You see, Tom, whatever lesson I teach you today, I am going to always come back and remind you of the need to climb all these eight Trees. You cannot have lasting success in one if you are not reaching for and climbing the others. Which means that you can still fail in the career that you love if you neglect the other areas of your life."

"Really?"

"Yes, Tom. Being good at your work and having a passion for it does not always guarantee success. Let me tell you about a young man I recently met, who was failing at a career that he was very talented at. His name is Simon.

"Simon had always wanted to be an actor and admirably pursued that passion. He went to acting school and was fortunate to have a family that supported him.

"Simon's father is a good friend of mine. I met him one day when I was photographing an amazing thunderstorm near the coast. His car had broken down and he was parked on the side of the road. I spent a couple of hours keeping him company while he waited for assistance. In those two hours we formed a friendship. He called me a couple of weeks later and asked me if I would talk to his son Simon and give him some advice.

"When I first met Simon, he was ready to quit on his dream. He had been attending auditions for a year and a half, but had failed to secure even one part. The thought of quitting saddened him but he also started to feel incapable. He started to doubt whether he had a genuine talent."

I would feel the same, I thought.

"What happened to Simon?" I asked. "Did he quit or did you get him to change his mind?"

"I am glad to say that Simon is still an actor. In fact, he is a successful one now. He has recently secured a few lead roles in the theatre and some minor roles in movies."

"What did you teach him? How did he succeed?"

"I taught him what I am teaching you, Tom," he grinned. "You see, just because we have not yet succeeded in our field of dreams, it does not mean we should replant ourselves in another field where we most likely do not belong. It just means that we have not appropriately nurtured ourselves in that field.

"The mistake Simon made was not in the Tree of Work. He was certainly trying very hard. His problem was that he was neglecting one of his other Trees of Life."

"Which one?"

"The Tree of Health. He did not lead a wholesome lifestyle. He was smoking cigarettes and not exercising. He was going out to too many parties and not sleeping enough. This affected his performances. His low energy levels made him lacklustre. The people assessing him noticed it. So whilst he had talent, he did not have completeness. He appeared insincere and unreliable.

"I told Simon that the best actors in the world take very good care of themselves. He listened and made a few adjustments that made all the difference in his performances. He started to wake early to exercise. He stopped smoking and started eating fresh fruit and vegetables. He started to look better and feel more energetic, which came out in his auditions."

The old man paused and leaned a little closer and whispered, "There is one other secret I taught Simon that made a world of difference. You see, after meeting Simon and hearing the story of his failing career, I realised that he was not thinking properly before his auditions. He was so worried about getting the part that he completely forgot to play it. So I taught him a powerful way to control his thoughts. I taught him the Circle of Conscious Living."

The old man sparked my curiosity.

"What is the Circle of Conscious Living?" I asked.

"It's the simplest way to master your thoughts and feelings, Tom," he smiled at me as if he was not going to say much more. But I had a feeling that I would soon be finding out.

4. Blend work with your personal life

"The next lesson I want to share with you, Tom, is very important because it makes it easier for you to achieve success at work without neglecting the other areas of your life. This lesson will save you lots of time and energy, which are your most valuable resources."

"You see this Tree of Work?" he asked and looked up. "It shares something in common with the Tree of Love. When you spend too much time in it, you spoil the work. You will *spoil* the enjoyment that work brings.

"Remember what I told you earlier about my working life. One of my deepest regrets was spending too much time at work and in a job I did not love."

"I don't understand," I interrupted. "If you did not love your work, why did you spend so much time there? Couldn't you have just gone home when you finished your work for the day?"

"You are absolutely right, Tom. I should've left for home, but I stayed back at work to impress my boss. I wanted my boss to know me better than my colleagues so I could be treated favourably and be first in line for a promotion. The problem was, everyone at work had the same idea. It turned into one big competition to see who got to work first and who left last."

"Who won?"

The old man laughed, "You are very competitive, Tom. The truth is, nobody won. We all lost. Even my boss lost because he had people working for him who did not really care for customers, because they were all too busy worrying about themselves."

"So everyone worked back late and missed out on seeing their families?"

"Yes Tom, on most days that's what happened."

"When my friends and I finish school and need to do

homework, we usually go to each other's homes to study. We don't stay at school past the bell. We take turns visiting each other and sometimes we have dinner together."

"That sounds great, but I could never have done that with my colleagues."

"Why not?"

"Because we were not *real* friends at work. We indulged in small talk and pretended to care about each other's families, but we never did get to meet them. You see, Tom, some adults are afraid to invite their work colleagues over to their place. They are afraid to open up their hearts and their homes to the people they work with. I spent hours upon hours with my work colleagues but was afraid to invite them into my own home."

"Why?"

"As I said earlier, I did not love my work, so the last thing I wanted to do was invite people over from work to continue talking about it. I also did not want my colleagues to see me as my true self at home. I was afraid that if they saw the soft side of my character as a family man, they would take advantage of me at work.

"How wrong I was, Tom. I now realise that to make real friends at work, you have to be yourself. You need to be open to genuine friendships with the people you come into contact with. To do that, you must have your real character on display at all times."

He paused, seeing that I was confused and asked, "What's the matter, Tom?"

"What do you mean by being yourself? Who else would you be?"

"I can see why you may be bewildered. A big mistake many adults make is that they do not act themselves at work. They act like somebody else."

"Like who?"

"You watch television don't you? You know that the people on television are acting in character."

"Yes."

"Well at work, we acted like that too, except we wrote the script for our own character. And the script went something like this: 'Must get respect at work by sounding serious and important. Must get respect by not showing or displaying my true feelings.'"

The old man said this in a robotic voice. I giggled.

"I think I get it, but why would anyone act like that?" I asked.

"We acted like that because we thought that sounding important was a way to get noticed. But do you know what? It takes a lot of effort to play a character all day. It saps your energy because you cannot just relax, let go and be yourself.

"When you hide your true feelings, you also hide your natural, fun personality; you hide who you truly are. All the friends I made during my working life were not real friends, because I never let them in close enough to see the real me!" he exclaimed.

I too sometimes felt that I had to act a certain way in front of some boys at school. I was too scared to be myself. I acted a lot tougher around them to make sure they would not pick on me. Work must have been a little like that.

"What should I do when *I* start working?" I asked.

"For starters," he said, "never apologise for loving your work. There are those who make a habit of complaining about their job. Be the opposite, Tom. Express how privileged you feel and how grateful you are to be serving others. Secondly, you should smile often. Smiling is the quickest way to let people know that you are *real*. People will not listen to you or follow you or share their vision with you if they do not *connect* with you and relate to you. And the easiest way to make that connection is to smile.

"Along with smiling, you have to speak truthfully at work. Say what's on your mind. There were many times I sat in meetings and did not speak up when I thought something was a bad idea. I agreed with others just to be popular and to make it easier for myself. But that was a way of lying to the people I worked with. People appreciate honesty, not popularity, Tom. Be truthful by speaking up and expressing your thoughts and ideas.

"You must also make sure that what you say is energetic and enthusiastic. The quality of your communication is very important. It ensures that your thoughts and feelings are congruent, so there are never any misunderstandings.

"I assure you Tom, that when you are genuine at work, you will make lots of friends. You will attract people like you who are also genuine. And they are the type of people you want to introduce to your family and to your other friends. Then you can start *blending* friendships in all areas of your life."

Life Blending

"Blending? What do you mean by that?" I asked.

"Let me ask you. Do you agree with me when I say that to live a complete and happy life, we need to be constantly climbing each of these eight Trees?"

"Yes."

"Well it takes a lot of time and energy to do that if you have to climb each one individually. The branches on these Trees overlap for a very good reason," he pointed at them.

"Life has become so complex and so fast that to balance every area is near impossible. If you add up all the time needed to eat healthy, exercise, relax, learn, work, hang-out with friends and family, create wealth, and give time to charity, you will soon realise that there are not enough hours left in the day to be even doing the other mundane tasks like brushing your teeth, buying groceries, driving to work and running errands. So balancing all these areas of your life is just not realistic. People try and separate all areas of their life in their pursuit to achieve balance. They do this for the reasons I mentioned earlier. They do not love their work and they are not authentic at work. They have no choice but to separate and try to balance all areas of their life because they act differently in each of them. They have a face for work, a face for family and another for friends. They have to step in and out of character every time.

"All these eight Trees should make up who you are, Tom. They are not separate versions of you. You should be the same at work as you are with family and friends. As I said earlier, work defines who you are as a person. It is an expression of your talents and forms part of your thoughts and feelings. It makes you an interesting person to talk to. So you should not ever be afraid to blend all areas of your life. And having genuine friendships at work is a great way to do that."

"Can you give me examples of how I can blend my life?" I asked.

"Certainly. Studying or working with a friend is one way. Going for a jog with that friend you study or work with is another, because you will be improving your health while fostering a friendship. If you talk about your work with that friend, during the jog, you will also be learning and coming up with ideas about your work. In other words, you will be climbing the Trees of Work, Friendship and Health all at the same time.

"There are so many other ways you can blend your life. By blending, you save many hours in your day and this makes living a complete life easier to achieve."

I started daydreaming of ways I can start blending all areas of my life, when the old man suddenly interrupted my thoughts with a compelling question.

5. *Don't work on time, work on results*

"Do you like going to school, Tom?"

"I guess so," I replied. The truth was that most mornings I did not want to go to school. It was a daily struggle to get out of bed.

"Is there anything you do not like about school?"

"Well, I have to do things when the teachers tell me to, when I'd rather be doing something else," I answered.

"I understand how you feel. When we finish school, we think that we will have more freedom to do what we want and when we want. But in reality, the workforce is just like school."

"Really?"

"Yes, we still have to adhere to strict time schedules that make us feel like our freedom is lost. And when our freedom is lost, our creativity is lost too. When that happens, passion for what we do abandons us, along with the potential to innovate.

"We are not machines, Tom. We cannot just switch on whenever we are ordered to produce good results. Warren from the fig orchard does not rush his fig trees to provide good fruit. They produce when they are ready. They have their own inner clock that is connected to nature. All he does is provide the right conditions for them to grow.

"We are no different. The best fruit of our work is produced when we are allowed to work in harmony with our own inner body clock. Not the clock on the wall! You will notice that I do not wear a watch. I stopped wearing one when I retired."

"But how do you know what time to wake up, what time to work and what time to go to bed?"

"Can I answer your question with another question? How do the birds know when to rise? How do the ants know when to work? How do the horses and the sheep know when to eat? How do the bees know when to get busy? They do not wear watches, but they all know what to do and when to do it.

We are no different to them."

I giggled at the thought of bees wearing watches around their little feet.

I also thought about how my dog, Woody, would wait for me at the same time every day after school.

The old man then advised, "When you grow up and start working in a job you love, focus on achievement rather than the amount of time you spend at work. Focus your mind on producing results and time will become irrelevant."

As I thought about putting my Mickey Mouse watch in my wardrobe forever, I became curious about what the old man said about our inner body clock.

"How can our bodies have an inner clock? That sounds weird," I laughed.

"It's not so weird, Tom," he chuckled.

"Our energy is critical when we work. We cannot work with enthusiasm if our body is not energetic. Our energy is connected to nature, which has its own time-keeping that is ruled by the sun and the moon. It tells us when to eat, when to work, when to rest and when to sleep. If we do not go with the flow of nature's time, our body will lose energy and our mind will lose focus.

"The biggest mistake I made at work was that I did not focus on producing results. I hid behind the clock on the wall. I worked long hours, only to produce mediocre results. Had I worked according to my own time, I could have achieved much more in less time.

"So if you work according to your body clock, Tom, you will have incredible energy and produce fine results. Results are what it's all about. Not time. That is my advice to you. Work when you are inspired. Rest when you are tired. Eat when you are hungry. Exercise when your body is restless and in need of motion.

"Working in this way might feel strange to you when you see others working by the clock. It might even make you fearful because you will feel the pressure to accrue hours, rather than focus on results. But you must remember to run your own race. Recognise that this feeling is nothing more than the fear of failure disguised as the need to conform."

Even though I had never worked before, I was wondering how it would be possible for me to work whenever I wanted. I could not imagine what would happen if the students at my school were allowed to work when they wanted. There would be chaos.

"The kids at my school would run riot if they were given that freedom," I said.

"You are right, Tom. If you do not love what you do, then you will most likely squander that freedom. But loving what you do fixes everything.

"If our schools and our places of work focused on fostering and nurturing our talents, we would not need anybody to tell us what to do and when to do it. We would take responsibility for our own work. We would not squander that freedom.

"There will come a time in your future when schools will have to give students more freedom to choose what they want to learn at a time and in an environment that caters to them individually. What a wonderful day that will be. I am hoping that the way we work will eventually drive and change the way schools teach. I also hope that I am still alive to see such a day. If not, then maybe you will spread this message for me after I am gone."

"Of course I will," I replied. "It sounds wonderful. Do you think it will happen soon?"

"Yes Tom, it is happening more and more everyday. I hear so many stories of people who have abandoned the clock to focus on results and lead a more intuitive life. Even younger people have become wiser. Young adults, like my daughter Penny, have experienced firsthand what time-driven working did to their parents' lives. Penny saw what it did to me. She has now chosen a career that gives her meaning and the freedom to work when she wants. She is an artist. She paints when she feels inspired. She sells her artwork as a way of seeking confirmation of her talent. It is not just about money anymore, Tom. It is not about how big your home is or how many cars you have. It is about living with energy, with passion and with friendships. It is about living life in all these eight Trees."

The old man looked up at the Trees with his eyes wide open. It was as if they were the source of his wisdom. Perhaps they were.

6. Slow down

He looked back down at me with a great big smile that warmed my heart.

"Nothing great has ever been done with haste, Tom," he continued, "so my next piece of advice to you is to slow down when working because speed will kill your creativity and will affect your ability to produce good results.

"I know this because that's what happened to me. I made the mistake of working with haste. My company set such high sales targets that I had no option but to work *faster* as well as longer; not just to meet these targets but also because the competition at work was so fierce.

"Working faster was supposed to help me get ahead but after many hectic years, I realised that working faster was nothing more than a false economy."

"What does that mean?" I asked.

"It means that I was like a dog chasing its tail," he chuckled. "The faster I worked the faster everyone else worked, including our competitors. Higher expectations were then set by the company. So instead of working less we still had to put in the same long hours, except this time with speed. And do you know who suffered, Tom?"

"Your family?" I asked.

"Yes, indirectly. It affected *me* first of all. And like I explained earlier, what affects me ultimately affects my family.

"My *health* suffered because I was not taking the time to eat my lunch slowly and rest throughout the day. Often I would eat lunch at my desk and gulp it down. My energy would dip throughout the day and by the time I arrived home I was exhausted.

"This fast pace at work then affected my personal life because it was virtually impossible for me to slow down when I arrived home. This had disastrous consequences on my relationship with Penny and Sarah."

I realised at that moment why the old man had such trouble connecting with his family. He was too impatient.

"There were other people who also suffered as a result of my speed at work," he continued.

"Who was that?"

"My customers. The fast pace of working made everyone at work stressed and cranky. We had less patience for our customers. We hurried through our consultations and did not listen to them attentively.

"Let me tell you something, Tom. When customers sense that you do not care, they will stop connecting with you. And when you lose that connection they will leave you and go to another business that does care."

"Is that what happened at your work? Did you lose customers?"

"Yes we lost a lot of good customers. But our company was so big that the impact was not felt immediately. Our company advertised to get new customers in through the front door whilst losing them out the back door. So the company was also like a dog chasing its tail. It was no longer moving forward. It was losing just as many customers as it was gaining."

"That sounds crazy. You should've all slowed down."

"We tried to but it was difficult to hit the reset button because our company was so big. Staff would leave before we had a chance to make any changes. The smart ones left because they recognised that they could not sustain such a fast pace. They looked for greener pastures. The not-so-fortunate ones simply burned out. The company then hired new staff that performed well for a little while. But once they too started working with speed they experienced the same problem. Whenever we had meetings to go through poor sales results, we would look to point the blame at certain people in the company, especially the ones that had left. Nobody ever thought of blaming it on *speed*. Speed was the problem and no one ever thought to apply the brakes.

"So you see, Tom, speed at work will actually lower your performance and make you ineffective. That's why I call it a false economy. You do not gain anything from speeding up."

Whilst I could not fully appreciate all that the old man said, I did however understand the need to perform tasks without haste. My mother always reminded me to slow down when I hurried through certain chores at home. Maybe my mother would make a good boss, I thought. I also thought that maybe adults would slow down if they actually loved their work.

7. Work all your life

"You know what else is important to learn about in this Tree of Work, Tom? You should never stop climbing it," the old man said with a firm and determined voice. "I made the mistake of retiring and doing no work whatsoever, like it was a way of reclaiming my life. In truth, it was one of the worst decisions I ever made. I don't think that any of us should ever stop working, at any age. Otherwise retirement becomes a barren field where old people are left to wither.

"The time I spent when I first retired was the most depressing of my life. After the golf games and the hours of gardening, my heart yearned for a new passion and my mind craved challenge and stimulation.

"When I look back on it, I realise that the company I worked for encouraged me to retire. They did not force me to, but it was often and subtly suggested. I was made to feel like I was slowing them down. New management consultants were hired and they pushed for higher sales targets with even fewer staff, which meant longer working hours. I simply could not keep up. My health was failing because of the long hours I had worked my whole life, so I had no option but to retire. I had to make way for someone younger and faster. Someone who was once like me! Someone with energy to burn, but who was naïve enough to work twelve-hour days, on the promise of making lots of money."

The old man paused for breath.

"The point I am making, Tom, is this. Why was I encouraged to retire? I could have been a huge asset to that company if they had helped me to reinvent myself to become a teacher at work. If I could share with them what I am sharing with you I could have improved their team morale and ultimately their performance. Instead, they hired consultants who were there one day and gone the next.

"I was there for thirty-seven years! I knew the company like the back of my hand. If they kept me in that field and nurtured me, I could have produced stunning fruit for them."

The old man shook his head in disbelief. He then shrugged it off, smiled and said, "*You know*, my friend Warren gets the best fruit from his older trees. He also gets to plant a lot of new trees from the older ones. The older fig trees have the best root system that has taken years to spread into the soil. They know the field well and know how to survive in it. Warren is a smart farmer. He takes grafts from the old fig trees and plants them into new fields to increase the size of his orchard. That is why he has one of the largest orchards in the world. He knows and utilises the value in those old fig trees."

The old man gazed out into the meadow, his eyes reflecting the distant past. His face, bright and calmly happy. Somehow he looked younger.

I realised that he just finished the seven lessons on working. I felt lucky to know them. I made a point to remember the importance of planting myself in the right field when I became an adult. I wondered what that field might be and felt a little restless to find out. I reminded myself that I was still just a boy and had plenty of time. I did not anticipate that I would find out what that was before the end of my time with the wise old man.

CHAPTER 7

Tree of Friendship

*"Wishing to be friends is quick work,
but friendship is a slow ripening fruit."*

Aristotle

The old man invited me to walk with him to the next tree in the circle. It was the Tree of Friendship and one that I was looking forward to. He asked me to sit underneath the branches and wait for him while he walked over to a nearby stream to collect some water. While I waited, I lay on my back and looked up to take in the branches of the eight Trees that danced in a circle around me. They looked magical from this viewpoint. As I looked at each one, I found myself recalling the stories and the lessons the old man had been sharing with me.

He returned from the stream with a small flask filled with water that we both shared.

We sat and settled as he started telling me about the next stage of his life.

"When I retired from work I found myself excited about not having to wake up early every morning. But as the days went by, I became bored and unhappy at home. Most days I walked around the house in my pyjamas, snacking and watching television. I had nothing to do. I realised that because I had spent most of my life working, I had forgotten how to enjoy the other areas of my life.

"I did not know where to look for meaning. Sarah had been living a much more complete life than I, so we had nothing in common. We were like strangers living in the same house. We had nothing interesting to say to each other and even worse, we did not know how to spend time together. It was at this time that Sarah and I parted ways. After that my life became completely empty and without excitement. I had failed to keep up with what was going on in the world of art, music, fashion, dance and world affairs. I began to think that this is what happens when people get older. 'I am old,' I told myself. And I accepted that as the way old people lived.

"When I was at work all those years, I thought that retirement would be my chance to start living an exciting life. But with my health failing and no idea of what to do with my time, I became very unhappy."

He lowered his head and added, "If only somebody had told me about these eight Trees in my youth."

The old man then turned to me and smiled, as if to put aside a bad memory.

The Epiphany

"But one day the course of my life was changed forever. Something happened to me that finally made me wake up to myself and opened my eyes to the wisdom that I am now sharing with you."

"What happened?" I asked.

"I hit rock bottom, Tom. I suffered a heart attack and went into hospital for a very long time. I became bed ridden and lost my will to live."

He then paused and added in a hushed voice, "Something mysterious happened to me in that hospital; something that I can only describe but cannot explain."

"What?" I asked with curiosity.

"Early one morning, as I lay in my hospital bed, a bright light woke me from a strange restless sleep. I assumed it was the morning sun so I tried to open my eyes but couldn't. I tried to move my arms and legs but couldn't. I became very agitated and frightened but could not speak. I was paralysed and powerless. I was confused and could not figure out whether I was dreaming or not."

I could relate to what the old man was describing. It must have been similar to the feeling I had when I woke up lost in the meadow. The difference however, was that I could open my eyes and move my body.

"I finally stopped trying to move and let my attention fall on the brightness," he continued. "It was then that I felt the warmth of the light on my face. It was calming and comforting. After a few minutes, I heard a soft and gentle voice inside my head. The voice told me where to find purpose in my life. It told me about my own eight Trees and pointed out the ones I failed to climb. It told me about all the mistakes I made. Although this filled me with regret, I started seeing my mistakes very clearly. It was at that moment that I found meaning, Tom. And to think, even at my old age!"

I sat totally absorbed and curious. I tried to imagine the voice that spoke to him and wondered who it could have been. Was it God?

"Did you find out whose voice it was that spoke to you?" I asked.

"No Tom I didn't," he replied. "I didn't need to. It was what the voice told me that was more important. After the bright light faded away, I was finally able to open my eyes and move my body. I sat up and smiled for the first time in a long time. I realised five things I needed to attend to immediately in my life. Firstly, I realised that I had to look after my health. Secondly, I realised that I needed to reconnect with Sarah and Penny. Thirdly, I realised that I needed to keep working and achieving meaningful goals in my life; goals that I was passionate about. Fourthly, I needed to develop a strong mind. Fifthly, I needed to nurture real and genuine friendships."

Importance of Friendships

"When I retired I realised for the first time that I was lonely. I knew people, but none I could call close friends. Yes I did reach the top in my career, but it came at a price; a price not worth paying. Not only did it cost me my health and my relationship with Sarah and Penny, it cost me many friendships. I neglected the friends I made during my years at school and university. And I never developed any genuine friendships during my working years."

He sat up straighter, pointed to the trees above us and said, "There's a very good reason why the Tree of Friendship is planted between the Tree of Work and the Tree of Learning in this circle. Notice how there branches overlap. It's because most of our friends come from the people we meet during our learning years and the people we associate with during our working years.

"Everyone needs friends, Tom. Friends bring laughter and joy into our life. True friends also help us to be ourselves. We tend to drop our guard and stop pretending to be something we are not. We are more relaxed and true to our character."

Importance of Integrity

The old man's voice turned a little grave when he next said, "But I have a word of warning. Having close friends in your life is rewarding but it can also be damaging if you do not act with the utmost of integrity."

"What does integrity mean?" I asked.

"Let me explain it by telling you a story that serves as a lesson on the importance of having integrity, especially when it comes to friendships at work.

"During my career I was given the opportunity to create and build a new business for the company. To do this I was partnered with a manager from another division. From the moment I met my partner we hit it off. We spent a lot of time together and could not help but develop a close friendship – one that was genuine and real. We launched the business with much fun and excitement and before long it was thriving. We achieved great success both in terms of our company's growth and our own careers. We were innovative. Our team was focused and happy. Our customers were delighted. We developed great ideas and implemented them with passion and enthusiasm. For a period, we were flying high in our industry. Life was grand for both of us. We celebrated and laughed often together and shared this friendship with our families."

He paused.

"But then, success got to our heads. We started to bicker and that eventually led to the end of our friendship."

"Why did you bicker?"

"I can't speak for him and what he may have done wrong but I do know what I did wrong, Tom. And that's all that matters, because it is to thine own self you must be true.

"I took my friend for granted and put my personal financial gain ahead of our friendship. I did not act with integrity.

"Initially the excitement of our alliance was enough to keep me energised and positive. But after many months of intense working, I became stressed. This caused me to become abrupt, irritable and intolerant and, in turn, argumentative. I became very competitive and selfish. I started setting unrealistic goals for the business and insisted that we work 'round the clock to achieve them. I developed a big ego and took myself too seriously.

"My ambitions to be the leader at work made me insensitive to my friend's feelings. I was not prepared to share leadership with him. I made him feel like he was more important to me as a colleague than a friend and I pushed him to the point where he started to neglect his own family, like I did mine.

"After a while, I am sure he decided to treat me in kind because that is human nature, Tom. We tend to treat people the same way they are treating us. A vicious circle of hatred developed between us, which poisoned our performance at work. What was once a friendship turned into a nasty battle for leadership. After many months of bickering, he decided to leave the company.

"Many times I thought about picking up the phone and resolving it with an extended hand of friendship, but pride and fear of rejection kept me from doing that. In the end, we both lost something really great. We lost the power of our friendship and our positive alliance – something that comes along only occasionally in life."

The old man turned to face me like he was bringing his attention back to the present moment and said, "So my advice to you Tom, is this – never argue with a friend if the cost of winning the argument comes at the expense of the friendship. Whatever you are fighting over is never worth that loss. I would gladly give up any financial gain that I now have, just to be friends again. The fun and laughter we shared would be remembered long after the money was spent and forgotten.

"My *other* advice to you, is to never lose sight of your eight Trees of Life. Spending time in each of them keeps you focused on your health, your love, your family, your work, your friendships, your learning, your wealth and your charity. When you are focused on all these areas, your positive qualities shine through and friends begin to see and experience the real you. That's what makes you a good friend. A friend with integrity."

The old man stopped to reach for the flask of water, took a sip and made a loud 'ahhh'. He winked with a smile and continued with enthusiasm. It looked like he was enjoying talking to me about the importance of friendship.

How to Be a Good Friend
"Tom, my next piece of advice to you about this Tree of Friendship is that, to gain and keep good friends, *you* have to *be* a good friend."

"How do I do that?" I asked. This was an important topic for me.

The old man's response was interrupted by a flurry of birds in the trees above us. We both looked up to watch them darting around and squawking. They looked like they were playing hide and seek as they zipped in and out of the branches.

He looked back at me and said, "To be a good friend, you have to be a fun person to be around; the type of person that makes others smile and laugh. Your friends will then keep that impression of you, even when you are not with them. The thought of you will bring a smile to their face."

"How can I be a fun person? Do I tell jokes?" I asked.

"You do not have to try too hard, Tom. Endeavour to always find a way to smile and laugh. Laughter is contagious. Whenever possible, be a happy and positive person."

He chuckled, tousled my hair and added, "Help your friends see the lighter side of life and not take themselves too seriously.

Nobody wants to be around someone who always takes themselves and life too seriously. Life is to be enjoyed and friends are there to help us do that.

"There is always reason for laughter. And we should never wait for the idea of a perfect life to start laughing. In fact, laughter is a way to deal with life's struggles.

"After my heart attack I would often visit comedy clubs to laugh and meet new friends. And do you know what? I am certain that laughter helped me mend my heart. I started to feel so much better. I found that laughter is something all humans crave. It brings people together.

"I met many friends at the comedy club, one of whom is Peter, a comedian I now consider a close friend. Peter told me that he had a very rough childhood. His father was very sick and his mother died when he was sixteen years old. He would often arrive home from school and find no food to eat. Peter had to virtually raise himself from that age. He was close to tears on most days and he lost all drive to go to school and continue his education. But Peter found happiness in himself because he remembered that he loved comedy; he loved to laugh and as a child he loved to make other people laugh. He told me that laughter makes all his sadness fade away.

"I visit Peter often at the comedy club and we always have a laugh together. He tells me the funniest jokes."

"I love to hear jokes," I said, "I love to laugh."

"So do I, Tom. *So – do – I*," he replied, grinning from ear to ear as if he was imagining one of Peter's jokes.

"So what else can I do to be a good friend?" I asked.

"Support your friends," he answered. "If a friend is feeling down or insecure, be the first to encourage them. Remind them of their positive qualities and help them to discover their goals and dreams. We all have insecurities and fears. A good friend helps us overcome them."

I remembered that my friends and I did in fact support each other on the soccer field; especially if one of us made a mistake. It never occurred to me that we could also be supportive *off* the field.

Hold True to Your Standards and Beliefs

I started imagining supporting my friends as the old man suggested. Deep down however, a part of me wanted my friends to like me for all the wrong reasons. I wanted to be popular.

It was at that instant that the old man looked at me intently, as if to read my mind and said, "But remember this, Tom. Only support your friends if it does not compromise your standards and beliefs."

"What are standards and beliefs?" I asked. It was the first time that I had heard such words.

"You will discover them in these eight Trees of Life," he promptly responded. "But you will not find them on the branches. In fact, you will not even find them above the ground. They lie beneath the surface, just like the roots of these amazing eight Trees that draw water from the nearby stream."

Sensing my confusion the old man smiled at me and added, "Standards and beliefs are the foundation of your character, Tom. It is what you stand for. A wise man once said that if you do not stand for something, you will fall for anything. Likewise, *you* must stand for something in your life. The more you do so, the deeper your roots will grow to give you stability in life. Your strength comes from connecting with them. You will then withstand any storms that blow your way. Some winds of change might bend and break the branches on these eight Trees but your roots below the ground never die. They remain hidden and protected. They do not feel the struggle or the storm. They are unmoving and serene. They fortify all that is above ground, ensuring that you grow from these tough experiences."

From what the old man was saying, I understood that I must be true to myself and not follow my friends blindly, even if it meant not being popular with them. I needed to stand strong and not join them if they were doing something I knew to be wrong.

As I thought about what he said, I realised that I did not have a clear idea of what I stood for. So I asked, "How do I know what my standards and beliefs are?"

"I urge you to look up to your Trees of Life for the answer to any of life's questions, Tom. You and I will soon part but the wisdom I am sharing with you remains here in these eight Trees. Their wisdom lives in your future and not in my past."

I looked up again, for an answer to the questions going through my mind. The leaves on the trees shone brightly in the sun, as they rustled in the gentle breeze. My heart filled with strength every time I gazed up at them.

I looked at the Tree of Love and noticed the Braided Branch that reminded me to love myself. I looked at the Tree of Family and remembered to love and support my family unconditionally. I looked at the Tree of Work and remembered that I must choose to love my work. I looked at the Tree of Learning and remembered that I must learn about all areas of my life. I looked at the Trees of Health, Wealth and Charity and knew that somehow they too would contain a profound wisdom soon to be revealed.

"These eight Trees hold your standards and beliefs, Tom," the old man revealed. "They are the guide by which you must live a strong and admirable life. As you grow older you must stay true to them by behaving according to their principles. If you believe in the Tree of Love, then you must show love towards others. If you believe in honouring and supporting your mother and father in the Tree of Family, then you must listen to and respect them. If you believe in the Tree of Health and the value of eating healthy and exercising daily, then you must not neglect your body by leading an unhealthy lifestyle. If you believe in the Tree of Work and the privilege of serving others, then you must work from the heart. If you value the Tree of Learning, you must not squander the opportunity to learn – you must seek out and read books that teach you how to live a complete life. If you believe in the Tree of Charity, then you must show daily acts of kindness towards others. If you believe in the Tree of Wealth and the freedom to live life on your own terms, then you must not squander your hard-earned money on frivolous purchases that bring you little in the way of lasting joy.

"These are just a few of the standards and beliefs that are common to everyone's Trees of Life. You must find more of your own that are specific to you. Whatever they may be, my advice to you is to never compromise them just to be popular with friends."

Choosing Friends Wisely

Being true to my standards and beliefs would be easier said than done. Some of my friends could be very persuasive and would sometimes dare me to do things I knew to be wrong. It would not be easy to stand up to those friends without appearing to be dull and boring. So I asked the old man, "What if my friends tease me for being a goody-two-shoes?"

"Appreciate that not everyone you meet is to be your friend, Tom. You must choose your friends wisely because the associations you keep will affect what you stand for.

"You must be careful not to be around those whose standards and beliefs contradict your own. You must regretfully avoid such friendships because they can poison the roots of your Trees of Life by tainting your thinking and your behaviour."

His comment reminded me of a saying my mother often used

when she warned me about befriending certain boys at school. 'One rotten apple spoils the whole bunch,' She would say.

"It is a fact, Tom, that we mimic our surroundings and the people we associate with. This is a phenomenon of human nature and a powerful force that shapes our standards and beliefs. And it is one that we can also use to our advantage. If you are going to model yourself on the people around you, make sure they are the type of people who inspire you to be your best. Make sure they are *worth* modelling.

"You must be wary that there are some people who may tease you when they see you focused on what truly matters in your life. They may try and mock your commitment. They may trivialise your achievements and try to bring you down to a standard that is not your own. Their mocking may not be obvious at first. It may be disguised as a joke that is aimed at making you feel uncomfortable for standing out from the crowd. It will put you under pressure to immediately jump back in with the crowd and dress like they dress, talk like they talk, walk like they walk and act like they act. You will do it without realising, and after a while, you will lose yourself and you will start to compromise your standards and beliefs."

The old man's advice made me feel a little guilty for choosing to hang around with a certain group of boys at school who were not very nice. They teased other students and disrespected teachers. I hung out with them sometimes just to be cool and out of fear that they might tease me if I did not join them. I always felt uncomfortable around them when they acted up but I never spoke out or avoided their company. I guess I was compromising my standards and beliefs.

As I was thinking this, the old man added, "If, however, you choose to spend time with friends who have similar standards and beliefs, you can reconnect with your own and make them even stronger.

"You will find lots of friends who have similar values if you go looking for them. Friends who take care of their health, friends who support and respect their families, friends who treat others with love and kindness, friends who value learning, and friends who have a strong work ethic."

The old man had me thinking about my friends. I realised that standing up for what I believed in may not make me the most popular boy at school but that did not seem to be as important anymore. He also made me realise that it was not about how many friends I had, but about the quality of those friendships.

Celebrating Differences

"Once you wisely choose your friends, Tom, my next advice to you is to accept them as they are. Do not try to change them. Appreciate them for their individual qualities. If you do not accept your friends as they are, they will start to act like someone else just to be around you. I am sure that you do not want to put that burden on them, do you?"

"No I wouldn't," I replied, relating to how I would feel if my friends did not accept me. "How do I show that I accept them as they are?" I asked.

"By being yourself around them," he replied. "If you are not yourself around your friends, they too will not act true to their character. They will see that you are not genuine."

He paused and added; "I think this is the reason for many conflicts around the world today. People fail to accept and respect other cultures. They make others feel uncomfortable to be different."

He stood up and gestured up to the tree, "If you look up at the Tree of Friendship, you will notice that it has three branches. Two branches represent friends from your learning years and your working years. The third branch however, represents your family friends. Not just your relatives but from the extended human family that dwell on this earth.

"If you look closely, Tom, you will also notice something special about this branch."

I too stood and looked up to notice the most unusual of branches.

"Wow," I said, "this branch has different coloured fruit. How can that be?" I asked.

"That's the wonder of the third branch on this Tree of Friendship," he responded. "Each fruit looks and tastes differently and yet is delicious in its own way. Each fruit represents the many different people living on this amazing world of ours."

The old man sat back down and reflected with a smiling face. "When I left the hospital and my strength returned, I decided to travel the world. This was the most exciting time of my life. I met so many people and made so many friends.

"I advise you to travel and experience other cultures regularly throughout your life, Tom. But remember that travelling does not mean staying at fancy resorts; they all look the same. It's getting out there to talk with the people in the community. It's dining in the same eateries and buying the local produce. When you interact with people from other cultures in this way, you will soon realise that everyone from all over the world want the same things: food, water, love and friendship. People want to be respected and appreciated. People want to share their story. People want to be friends!"

He paused and added, "It's a big world out there, Tom, with many diverse and rich cultures."

I interjected, "I have a friend at school who recently arrived from India. He tells me amazing stories of places I can only ever imagine. I go to his home often and we play together. My parents even visit and sometimes we all stay for dinner. The food his mother and father make is different yet so delicious."

"It sometimes takes children to bring adults together," the old man said. "Children from all backgrounds play beautifully together because they understand the universal language of fun and laughter. Children also play well together because they accept each other just as they are. That is a lesson that all adults can learn from."

"Really?"

"Yes, Tom. Most adults are not that accepting."

I thought about my friends and how each one was unique in their own way. That's what I liked about them. It made them interesting. They always managed to surprise me. The thought of adults not accepting other adults baffled me.

"Why do adults not accept each other as they are?" I asked.

"That is a good question. And the answer is the same as the one I gave you under the Tree of Work earlier. People are afraid to act themselves around others, especially when they are around people who look different or speak a different language. They feel that if they act in a friendly manner, they might become the target of unscrupulous conduct. They fear that they may get hurt in some way.

"It always comes back to fear, Tom. Fear is what keeps people from being genuine around others. Fear is what keeps them from walking up to a person and saying hello with a genuine smile. *Fear* is the enemy of friendship!

"Fear makes people irrational," he continued passionately. "Fear motivates prejudice. Fear makes you suspicious. You cross the street. You look down. You frown. The other person sees this and they too will frown and look down or walk the other way.

"Fear makes us hurt other people's feelings. Fear makes us turn a blind eye to other people's suffering. Fear strips us of our freedom. Ultimately, fear takes away our happiness."

The old man paused to catch his breath and added, "Do you

know what else I have learned about fear? It is almost always baseless. We rarely have a valid reason to fear. It is one thing to be cautious but another to be totally paralysed by fear to the point where it stops us from making new friends."

"I don't understand something," I interrupted. "If fear is so bad, why do adults give in to it?"

"Because they make generalisations about other people."

"What does that mean?"

"It means they prejudge someone without even knowing them. If, for instance, a school student about your age treated me rudely, would it be fair of me to think that all students your age were also rude?"

"Of course not, that would be silly."

"But that's what most people do every day, Tom. They make sweeping generalisations about others before they even meet them. It's like saying that all teenagers are angry and violent or all old people are grumpy. Rationally, we know that neither comment is true. I meet many teenagers who are kind, peaceful and polite."

"And I meet many older people who are not grumpy," I chimed in. "In fact they are usually kind and patient."

"That's right, Tom. So the lesson is this: we should never judge people before we meet them because when we generalise in our mind, we breed prejudice in our heart. Prejudice is what stops us from making new friends because we start to fear people before we even talk to them.

"To break that cycle of fear we must treat everyone we meet as individuals no matter their background, age, what clothes they wear, which school they go to, which church they attend, where they live, where they work, what food they eat or what music they listen to. We should not view their difference as an excuse to fear them."

"I think I know what you mean," I said. "We should not judge a book by its cover."

"That is precisely my point," he replied. "A lot of adults speak of *tolerance* when it comes to dealing with the problem of prejudice in our society. But this focus on tolerance is one of the causes of prejudice. It assumes there is something to tolerate about the other person. It highlights people's differences for scrutiny. Therefore it is not genuine or unifying.

"Travelling to other countries helped me to realise that true friendship is not about *tolerating* other people's differences. It is about *celebrating* them. When we focus on appreciating differences we start to develop a positive curiosity for others. I believe that half the fun is getting to share and enjoy each other's diversity. That's what I found to be the most enjoyable part of travelling. It was the differences in culture that sparked my interest in the people I met. My curiosity helped me to shed my fear, walk up to a person and introduce myself.

"When we act with curiosity and approach someone with a friendly smile, we break the cycle of fear and start a new cycle of friendship, one that can conquer fear."

He paused to look at me and asked, "Are you with me on this mission, Tom? If we both do this and teach others to do the same, we can start a new movement. After all, we are all on this Earth together."

He looked at me and smiled. I smiled back and felt a sense of pride to be a part of a team with a common purpose.

I kept on smiling because I also realised that the old man was becoming a friend, a friend with the same standards and beliefs.

*A*lthough I was lost in the woods on that day, it was this wisdom that the old man shared which helped me find a little piece of myself and the things that I would stand for in life. I knew from that moment, that I would live to recognise and never compromise my standards and beliefs, even if it made me unpopular or, even worse, ridiculed by others.

I certainly did not live a perfect life. I struggled to uphold my standards sometimes and compromised my beliefs at other times. But whenever I did, I had my eight Trees of Life to guide me back to my roots. I always returned to the wisdom and ensured that the roots of my Trees remained deep and strong.

CHAPTER 8

Tree of Wealth

The rich get richer.
The wise get wealthier.

*I*n my adult years I came to realise how accurate the old
man was about the next Tree in the circle. He told me that it
would be the easiest to climb but only if I lived a complete and
fulfilling life, otherwise it would prove to be the hardest.

He told me that wealth was important because it gives us the
freedom to live life on our own terms. It liberates us by opening
up our options for living. The consequence of such freedom is
daily happiness.

In my life I have learned that wealth, just like happiness,
is not something that can be pursued. Rather it is that which
effortlessly flows when we live a complete life filled with purpose.

The wise old man taught me that wealth is a state of mind
and not the state of one's bank balance. The difference has
a lot to do with what you invest in. What you invest in,

91

ultimately defines your wealth.

He taught me about the safest and most rewarding investment that would yield the most abundant wealth imaginable.

He taught me to invest in myself.

After the old man finished talking to me about the Tree of Friendship, he gestured to the next tree in the circle and started to walk over to it. I followed and could not help but notice a smile on his face; a smile that hinted I was about to learn another remarkable lesson.

I remembered which Tree we were up to and asked him: "Is this what people call the money tree? I want to learn how to make lots of money when I grow up. I want to be rich!"

"This is your Tree of Wealth, Tom," he answered, "but I would not call it the money tree. I prefer to call it the freedom tree."

Being Rich versus Being Wealthy

"Being rich and being wealthy are two different states. People may like to think that being wealthy is about having lots of money. But that is inaccurate. When you chase money, you lose your freedom; but when you pursue wealth, you will gain the ultimate freedom – the freedom to live your life without regard for money.

"Money flows from living your best life, Tom, and not the other way around," he added poignantly. "I used to think that I would start living an exciting life when I had enough money. My constant focus on finances was like a load on my mind that I carried around with me all day. I used to tell myself, 'When I pay off my mortgage and have more money, I will eat better, I will exercise, I will change jobs and do what I really love. I will spend more time with Sarah and Penny, I will read more books, I will go on more holidays, I will be a better person, I will be happy'. But this way of thinking killed my romance for life. It trained me for poverty rather than wealth and ultimately made me unhappy. I lived a poor life with money but no wealth."

"But you were rich," I said. "You had a big house in a nice neighbourhood. That's what I want when I grow older. Should I not want that?"

"There is nothing wrong with buying a big house in a nice neighbourhood if you can afford it, Tom. But if you have to borrow too much money for it, then it is not worth it. You will end up spending too much time working to pay it off. Where is the freedom in that? Making money to pay off a big debt is what I call real poverty.

"Some people make the mistake of spending a large portion of their money on just one expensive item. For example, I have come across many people in my travels with meagre incomes that make the mistake of buying an expensive car, even borrowing too much from the bank for it. If your finances are healthy and you are not sacrificing money from other areas of your life, then there is no problem in making such a purchase. However, if it means you have to eat poor quality food, then it is not worth it. If it means having to work too many hours to pay it off, it is not worth it. If it means spending less time with your family, it is not worth it. If it means having to go without some necessities for your home, it is not worth it. If it means not having enough time to play sport and hang out with friends, it is not worth it. If it means having to ignore others in need, then it is not worth it. I can give you many more examples of how spending too much on one area of your life can deprive you in other areas; and they all have one thing in common. They lead you to a life of poverty, not wealth.

"You see, Tom, this Tree of Wealth is the easiest to climb, but only if you invest in your health, love, family, friendship, work, learning and charity. True wealth comes when you *budget* and spend your time and money across all these areas."

I often heard my parents use the word 'budget'. They reminded my sister and I that food, clothing and having a roof over our head were their priorities. I wondered if my parents knew something about the Tree of Wealth.

"I want to tell you a story," the old man continued. "It is a story that will highlight the difference between wealth and money. It is a story about two families – one rich with money and the other, with meagre means and a modest lifestyle.

"One Sunday, the rich family decided to go out for lunch at a fancy restaurant that served great food exquisitely made by a well-known chef. They enjoyed themselves immensely and the experience cost them around four hundred dollars.

"The more modest family, on that same Sunday, travelled together to the local farmers market where they bought some organic produce, that cost them around forty dollars. They then went home and lovingly prepared a home-cooked meal. After they ate, they enjoyed the afternoon in the backyard playing ball games.

"Now, can I ask you one simple question? Which family do you think is the wealthier of the two?"

I thought I knew what the old man was getting at, so I replied, "They are both wealthy."

"Exactly, Tom. They both enjoyed a nutritious meal together that they both could afford. The family that spent forty dollars was none the poorer.

"*Now*, what if I told you that the family who went to the restaurant was not that rich after all. In fact, what if I told you that they had to sacrifice money from other essential areas of their life to be able to spend that much. Which family would you now consider wealthier?"

"The modest one, the one that spent only forty dollars," I replied.

"And *there* is the lesson, Tom. You must be clever when spending your money. You must ask yourself, can I achieve the same result without spending money needlessly? Adopting a simple lifestyle makes it easier to have that choice.

"Some of the smartest and wealthiest people with the most freedom and the most choices in life are the ones who save their money without neglecting to invest in themselves. They just do so frugally. You see, Tom, it is not how much you spend, but rather the return on what you spend. And it is often said that the simplest things in life are free. From experience, I would have to agree," he said nodding as if to agree with his own comment.

"Is there a way that I can have both money and freedom?" I asked.

"That's a very good question. Yes there is, and that's what this Tree of Wealth is all about. I have come across many successful people in my travels, and they all have one thing in common. They live life with a sense of freedom. They do not defer their happiness for the sake of making money. They develop an attitude that money will eventually come their way if they live a complete life. They wake up every morning and do the simple things consistently. They eat well, they exercise, they spend quality time with their family, they are constantly learning and improving, they love their work, they have fun with friends and they are kind and generous. They create wealth before they create money. Living a complete and happy life *is* their wealth."

"I did not expect *that* to be the lesson on this Tree of Wealth," I responded. "I thought you were going to teach me how to make lots of money."

"Well Tom, the irony of money is that you cannot be obsessed with it at the expense of freedom, otherwise you will never attain it. You must let it flow to you. The only way to do that is to live a complete life, which means investing in yourself first. Once you invest in yourself, you will start to attract money. Let me explain how this happens.

"If you look up you will notice that there are two branches on this Tree of Wealth. The branch on the left is where you save money and invest in things that will make it grow. The branch on the right is where you invest money in yourself. As you can see, the right one has the most fruit, spread equally over the whole branch, whereas the one on the left only has fruit on the highest part of the branch. But there is something else you will notice about both branches. Take a closer look," the old man directed my gaze.

I looked very carefully and squinted to see if there was some small detail I was missing. At first I didn't notice anything peculiar but as I started imagining climbing the tree, I noticed that the left branch looked very difficult to climb. It reached high up to the sky and had no climbing branches to cling to. It must have been the tallest of all the branches on all eight trees. One would feel rather free sitting on the highest point, I thought to myself. It also had lots of stunning fruit right at the very top, just as the old man had pointed out. But there was no fruit anywhere else along the branch.

I then noticed that the right branch initially forked away from the left one and curled back towards it higher up. To a climber like me, I knew that the best way to reach the amazing fruit on the left branch would be to first climb the one on the right.

It was at that moment that the old man began to explain the wisdom of climbing the right branch.

"To achieve real and lasting wealth, you must invest in yourself by climbing the branch on the right before you can reach the one on the left. Those who endeavour to first grow their money, without living a complete life in their eight Trees, can find the left branch perilous to climb.

"If, however, you invest in yourself first, you will easily reach the top of the left branch. Then, and only then, will you have both freedom and money."

Investing in Yourself

"How do I invest in myself?" I asked.

"The answer to that question, Tom, comes from knowing where and how you spend your time and money. If you spend them wisely it becomes an *investment*," he said with enthusiasm.

"What's an investment?"

"An investment is something that makes your wealth grow and multiply. For example, if I water this tree, it will grow and bear more fruit. This extra fruit is the return on my investment; it has grown *because* of my tending to it.

"If you want to become a doctor, you would invest your time and money studying to be a doctor. The return on your investment is not only the income you make when you start to work as one, but the satisfaction you feel when helping patients. If you want to become an artist, you would invest in buying the paint and canvas – you would also invest your time and energy in creating the artwork. The return on your investment comes not only when you sell the paintings for money but from the satisfaction of creating work that brings pleasure to people.

"So, what should I invest my time and money in?" I asked.

"Where do you think, Tom?" he asked and gestured upwards.

"In my eight Trees?"

"Precisely! Spending time and money on all these areas of your life is what I consider the best investment. Your return will be living a complete and happy life. And your performance in all areas will be outstanding. That's what helps you to experience the best kind of wealth, the kind that gives you freedom."

I scanned the trees above me and asked, "I think I know how to invest my time but how do I invest my money? Can you give me an example of what to do for each Tree?"

"Yes, I definitely can, Tom. It is not difficult to know how to spend your money if you remember one very important rule. Money is just like time. You must budget and spread it across all eight areas without neglecting any. To do that, you must not spend too much on just one area.

"In the Tree of Health you invest in your health by buying fresh wholesome food, exercising and relaxing. Your return will be a life of high energy. Now, it does not and should not cost much to invest in these areas. On the branch of exercise, for instance, ask yourself, 'Do I need to spend thousands of dollars on expensive gym equipment or will a pair of running shoes achieve the same result?' 'Should I pay money for gym membership or should I exercise in the park with friends?' The answer to these questions always comes back to how much money you have and what money you have left over for the other areas of your life.

"Likewise, in the Tree of Love, spending time with your sweetheart doing things that you both love does not have to cost much. Instead of going to a fancy restaurant, you can pack a picnic basket and sit in the park to enjoy it. Instead of going to the cinemas you can rent a movie or read a book together. Your return on investment will still be the same. You will be nurturing a close loving relationship.

"In the Tree of Family, you can all work together to keep your home tidy and clean. If you can afford it, employ help to maintain your home. If you cannot afford it, then don't waste money on services that you can do yourself. Likewise, if you can afford expensive furniture then buy and enjoy it. If you cannot, then what does it matter what chair you sit on when enjoying the evening meal?"

The old man was right and I began nodding.

He smiled at me and said, "Let me now tell you, Tom, about investing in the Tree of Work and the biggest mistake that most people make. When you are older and start working, this lesson will become very important.

"A lot of people work very hard so they can save money to invest on the *left* branch. They tell themselves that when they have enough money they will retire and live a happy life.

"It's good to save money but the mistake most people make is that once they save enough, they end up investing it in other people's dreams instead of their own."

"What do you mean by other people's dreams?" I asked.

"Well, some people forget to invest their hard-earned money in their own career or business. Instead, they invest it in large companies that are controlled by other people. I see many hard-working people make that mistake time and time again. They grow their savings and instead of reinvesting in their own business, they invest in someone else's."

"Why would they do that?"

"There are three main reasons, Tom.

"First, they are impatient. They want to make money quickly without having to work for it. They want to try and climb the left branch first.

"Second, some people do not discover their own field of dreams. They do not love their work so they see no point in investing in something that they do not love.

"Third, they invest in other businesses out of fear. They fear failing and losing their money so they try to pass that responsibility onto someone else. That way, if they lose money, they have someone to blame. I have seen that happen so many times over the years, especially when people invest on the stock market. Do you know what a stock market is, Tom?"

"Yes, I have heard my father say that he owns shares. He is

always worrying about whether they are going up in price."

"I understand your father's concern. I lost a lot of my money by investing on the stock market. And so I have learned that one should never invest time, energy or money in other people's dreams unless one also shares those dreams and is actively involved in making them happen. If you happen to work for a big business where you love your job and believe in the mission, then there is nothing wrong with investing in it. But if you have your own business, you should be investing in that first because that's where you will make the most money.

"If you are a chef, you could invest in better cooking equipment and kitchen facilities or you might open another restaurant. If you are a farmer, you could invest in machinery and irrigation systems that sustain your crop. If you are a builder, you could invest in the latest tools that make you more efficient and deliver better workmanship."

I thought of my father's construction business and understood what he meant.

"I think I have made my point very clear about investing in the Tree of Work. Let me now give you an example of investing in your Tree of Learning. I believe that you should always invest your time and money into expanding your knowledge. If your career is earning you money, then you should invest some of that money in courses that teach you new ideas. If you do not have enough money to spend on courses then you can always buy books. If you cannot afford to buy books then you can borrow them from the local library.

"Do you see what I mean, Tom? There are always affordable alternatives that achieve the same result. You do not need to have much money to live a wealthy life. True wealth is in these eight Trees and as long as you are investing what you can afford across all of them, you will live a wealthy life whether you accumulate money or not."

"But will I ever get to reach and climb the left branch?" I asked. I loved a challenge and the left branch looked difficult to climb. I felt like I had to conquer it. I especially had to get to the abundant fruit at the very top.

"Yes you will, Tom. I assure you that if you keep investing in yourself you will eventually reach a stage on the right branch where the top of the left branch is within reach. It is then and only then that money starts flowing to you."

"How can money just flow to you? You make it sound like it happens by magic."

"Good things happen to people who live by and invest in these eight Trees," he replied. "Some say that such people are just lucky, but I say that when you invest in all areas of your life, you put yourself in a position to take advantage of opportunities that come your way. When you live a complete life that makes you happy, healthy and loved, you start to develop a positive frame of mind and a warm attitude. This attracts good things and good people to you. And these often come with opportunities to work and invest in new ideas that excite you and make money for you."

"It does sound like a bit of magic," I said, smiling eagerly. He smiled back at me and winked as if to suggest that maybe there was.

I sensed that the lesson was over. I looked up to see what Tree in the circle we were up to. It was then that I realised that the old man had given me an example of investing in myself for all areas except one. So I said to him, "You forgot the Tree of Charity. Is that a Tree of Life I do not have to invest in?"

"You are observant, Tom," he replied. "There are no exceptions to investing in your life. The Tree of Charity is no less important than any other. When it comes to charity, the simple rule is to give what you can. If you have plenty of money, then share some of it with others who are in need. But if you do not have enough to spare, you can still be charitable in many other ways.

"In fact, let me now explain to you the best way of being charitable. You will see that it does not require any money at all."

CHAPTER 9

Tree of Charity

*"You give but little when you give of
your possessions. It is when you give of
yourself that you truly give."*

Kahlil Gibran

It was nearing noon as the sun reached higher in the sky. Instead of walking to the Tree of Charity, the old man asked me to walk with him into the open, grassy meadow. I wondered where he was going, until we arrived at a patch of yellow wildflowers. He knelt down and picked a few to create a posy.

"Do you like flowers, Tom?" he asked.

"Flowers are for girls," I responded shyly.

"Well *I* like flowers, Tom, and I am a boy!" he exclaimed playfully.

"I do like the flowers that grow around my grandmother's cottage," I said as we walked back to the eight Trees. "She has so many colours in her garden during springtime."

"Yes, I think that spring flowers are the most beautiful of all," he replied.

"You know, Tom, you don't have to be a girl to appreciate the miracle and the beauty of flowers. I find that when I look at them, my spirit is lifted; I feel happy. That's why I sometimes give flowers to others; I want to spread happiness and remind people of the beauty in the simple things on our wonderful planet."

"You pick flowers and give them to strangers?" I asked.

"Not strangers, Tom, neighbours or people I regularly see on my morning walks. Being kind and generous to others does not have to be complicated or grand. Placing flowers at a neighbour's front gate is one simple act of charity. It is my way of giving, in the hope that it lifts their spirits. It could be someone who is working very hard and needs to be reminded of the beauty of the world around them, or it could be someone who needs to have their faith in mankind restored. Who knows, you may even inspire them to do the same."

"How is the giving of flowers charity? Isn't charity about giving money?"

"That's what most people think," he replied.

We arrived back under the eight Trees and the old man reached out to hand me the posy of flowers. "Whenever you see flowers, Tom, I want you to remember the Tree of Charity.

"Flowers are a reminder that nature is charitable with us daily. It provides the most beautiful array of colour and asks for nothing in return. There is a lesson in that for us. The lesson is that true charity does not cost anything.

"Do you know why some people neglect this Tree? It is not because they are unkind. We humans, are innately charitable because we love to share. It is because some of us do not know *how* to share and *what* to share. We do not know what charity truly means. Most people think that charity is material; that it means giving money. If you are materially wealthy and you are in a position to give money to others and make a difference in their life, then that is wonderful. But if you do not have money to spare, then do not think for a minute that you cannot be charitable. This Tree grows in everyone's Garden of Happiness. Whether we are rich or poor, we all have the capacity to be charitable in one way or another."

He paused to gaze up at the tree and said, "The truest form of charity comes from the heart, not the wallet, Tom. It's the giving of our ourselves. We get to see and connect with the people we are helping. In fact I cannot think of a better way of being charitable than to give of myself to others in need. It is the best way I know how."

"How do you give of *yourself*? What does that mean?" I asked.

"Giving has many faces. You can give of your time, your words of encouragement or even a simple smile. Be perceptive; you will find that just listening to someone can be giving, if that is what the person needs the most."

Giving Is Receiving

"I have also learned that we get more out of being charitable than we ever put in."

"What do we get?"

"The most important thing we get, Tom, is the blessing of the person receiving our charity. Do not underestimate the power of good wishes bestowed upon us by the people we are charitable to. All the money in the world cannot measure the fulfilment we receive. It fills our heart with immense positive energy. Somehow, somewhere, sometime, someone will return that kindness when we most need it."

I understood what the old man meant about feeling good when helping others. There were times when I helped my friends at school with homework. There were other times when I shared my lunch with them. I always felt good about it because I loved to share my things; although it didn't feel like charity to me. Could charity be that simple?

I was curious about what the old man did to be charitable. So I asked him, "How do you show charity to others?"

"There are a number of things I try to do, but my favourite is to share the wisdom of the eight Trees with the people I meet in my travels. I think that sharing *ideas* and knowledge acquired during one's lifetime is a great way to be charitable. Sharing wisdom that can help others live a better life is very rewarding indeed. Your return will not only be the feeling of gratitude. Your return will come in many forms. It could be expanding your circle of friends, or simply being inspired by other people's triumphs.

"I also like to share my *time* and company with others who crave a social life, but who are often pushed to the edge of society. I do this by spending an evening each week volunteering at a shelter in the city, serving food to the homeless."

"Really?"

"Yes Tom. After food service, I get to sit and talk with some of them. They are grateful for the meal, but I think they are more grateful for the company."

The old man paused in reflection and said, "Let me tell you something very important. When you sit and eat with people, you develop a bond. It makes the meal more enjoyable and makes you and the other person feel valued and important enough to share a meal with. When I sit and eat with the people at the shelter, I try to make them feel like they are a visitor in my own home, because I believe that giving should not feel like charity to the ones who need it. It should feel like hospitality."

"I have seen some of those shelters in the city," I said. "Some of the people who visit there look very scary. How do you sit and eat with them?"

"Looks can be deceiving, Tom. Some people have been

through much hardship in their life and they only *look* scary. Also remember that when your charity is motivated by love, it does not matter who the recipient of that love is. In fact, the grumpy ones need our love the most," he laughed as he pulled a grumpy face. "I seek them out during food service. They are a little abrupt with me at first, but I stay true to my commitment of giving my time unconditionally through words of good humour. I keep smiling and that brings them around eventually. Never underestimate the power of humour to lift the human spirit, Tom. I have witnessed the grumpiest of people giggle like children when they hear a funny joke."

We both smiled and sat in momentary silence. I started to recall some jokes that my father would tell at the dinner table on most nights. I missed him and his happy face.

"What else do you do to be charitable?" I asked.

"Well, I also visit lonely elderly people in nursing homes," he replied. "It is one of the most rewarding things I do because the people I meet there are so appreciative of my time. Good company and a connection with others is what they crave the most. Giving material things to such people is useless, Tom. True charity is not about what you want to give but what the other person needs the most.

"I have found that the elderly are bursting with experiences and stories from their younger years. In fact, I have learned many interesting and valuable lessons just by listening to them. I sometimes feel it is *I* who is receiving charity."

He paused.

"Nursing homes can be very lonely places. It saddens me to say that my mother was in a nursing home when she died."

He paused again and looked down at his hands.

"One of the biggest tragedies in life is loneliness. Any human physical ailment can be managed, even poor health; but loneliness is very painful for the heart. Humans need humans, Tom. We need company as much as we need air to breathe. We need that connection with others. Without it, we die emotionally. And that is the saddest thing to witness."

His eyes became a little teary.

"My mother was my hero. I loved her more than anything else in the world. When my father died in his older years, she lived on her own. Losing my dad was very hard on her. I think her health started to fail from loneliness.

"I was so busy with my corporate life at the time that I was blind to her suffering. I told myself she must be okay because she was out of sight. I used to convince myself that she must be out socialising with friends. I made those assumptions without checking in on her, because it was my way of excusing my absence. Sure, Sarah and I did make an effort to visit, but sometimes we would go for weeks without seeing her. During this time she would sit alone and do nothing. She didn't even have the desire to make food for herself. She lost the motivation to live.

"I would sometimes call her from my office. She would put on a brave voice to make me feel better. I pretended to believe her because it gave me an excuse to stay focused on my work. But there were many hours of loneliness in between those phone calls, Tom. I took it for granted that she would always be around."

The old man's eyes welled up with tears as he continued, "My mother eventually became too sick to look after herself at home. We had to put her in a nursing home. She was never the same after that. Soon after, she died alone in her room.

"I received the call when I was in a boardroom meeting!" he said with angst.

He paused to compose himself but struggled to do so.

"She used to cradle me in her arms when I was a child. She was there for me when I needed her but I was not there when she needed me."

The old man choked back his last few words as tears trickled down his cheeks. My eyes also welled up as I imagined it to be my own mother. In that instant I vowed that I would never put my career ahead of my family.

"The way I neglected my mother during that time is the biggest regret of my life, Tom. I hope you never ever feel such pain in your heart."

He wiped his eyes and added, "I now visit nursing homes in memory of my mother. I sit and talk with the people there. They have many stories to share. I love to see their eyes come alive when they relate stories of exciting times in their life. But do you know what, Tom? Do you know what they talk about the most? They talk about their families.

"I live with the hope that maybe someone was also charitable with my mother when she most needed it in her final hours. I can imagine that she would have spoken about her family with pride. She was always very proud of us. And knowing her, she would have had enough love to forgive my absence. That was her own final act of charity towards me."

Chapter 10

Tree of Health

*Energy is the only true
measure of good health.*

*E*ven *as an eight-year-old boy, I knew the simple lessons
about good health. My father would remind me of the need
for good nutrition and physical training before every soccer
game. My mother would prompt me to rest and recharge after
it. What they did not know however, and what the old man
shared with me under the Tree of Health, was the most powerful
wisdom of all and one that has helped me live with vitality
throughout my life.*

*He told me that my body was full of energy. So when I
sometimes felt tired, it did not mean that my body lacked energy.
It meant that the energy was trapped inside of me, stagnant
and unreleased. The old man taught me the secret to releasing
it. He did this by showing me the energy compass of my life,*

which revealed the three other, often forgotten, energies. He also revealed to me their actual source. I discovered that they were not on the branches of the Tree of Health – they lay hidden beneath the surface, in my mind and in my heart.

The Three Branches of Good Health

I realised that the old man had just finished teaching me about all the eight Trees, except for the big one in the middle.

From the outside of the circle of trees, I could see the Tree of Health as the largest tree that supported all the others with its far reaching branches. It was midday and the sun was directly above us. It looked like you could draw a straight line upwards from the top of the tree to meet the sun. I could sense the old man looking too. He gestured for me to sit down beneath it.

We sat in momentary silence. I looked up and asked, "Why is this your favourite tree? You keep referring to it. It is also the biggest one in the meadow so it must have some special fruit on it."

"The fruit from the Tree of Health is the most important of all," he replied. "It sustains your body, Tom. And when you have sustenance, you will have plenty of energy to climb your other Trees of Life. Spending time on it will help you look better, feel better and be more productive in all of your daily activities. It will help you live longer and feel stronger. It is the single most important Tree of Life. That is why you must remember to focus on it and return to it throughout your day; otherwise you will pay the price of low energy and ill health. If that ever happens, it will be difficult for you to enjoy the fruit from the other Trees of Life.

"It is difficult to climb the Tree of Love if your focus is on an illness. It is difficult to climb the Tree of Family if you are physically unable to show your support. It is difficult to climb the Tree of Work if you are too tired to be productive. It is difficult to climb the Tree of Friendship if your fun and cheerful nature is dampened by low energy. It is difficult to climb the Tree of Learning if your weak body has weakened your mind. It is difficult for you to climb the Tree of Wealth if you are too tired to invest in yourself. It is difficult to climb the Tree of Charity if your illness has you focused inwards rather than outward on helping others. If you do not have your health, you have nothing!"

He paused to gaze upwards and said, "Look up, Tom, and tell me what you see."

I tilted my head to take in the breadth of the tree. I noticed three main branches that fanned out from the trunk. They spread out into many other smaller branches that were entwined with the branches of the seven other trees.

I looked back at the old man and said, "I see three big branches."

"That's right, Tom. The Tree of Health contains three very important branches that you must climb daily throughout your life. The first branch contains the fruit of nutrition that fuels your body. The second contains the fruit of exercise that builds your strength and stamina. The third is the branch of relaxation that helps you rest and recharge.

"I have left this tree until last because I want you to pay very close attention. Good health is probably something that you take for granted because you are still young. In youth, we can never conceive of the day when we become ill and lose our energy for a long time.

"There's a very good reason why you woke up on this tree, Tom. You have your health. You can always find your way in life because you still have the energy to take action in the direction of your goals and dreams. But as you grow older and consistently neglect this Tree, it gets harder to climb back up and eat from the fruit of good health. This Tree is not like the others. It is not as forgiving. When the momentum of ill health takes over, it is difficult to reverse. There was a period in my life when I neglected my health and lost my energy for a very long time."

The old man fell silent.

"Are you still sick?" I asked. "Is that why you carry that bottle of medicine with you?"

"Yes Tom," he replied, "I *was* very sick. I am much better now and well enough to stay out of hospital if I stay focused on living a complete life. At one stage, I thought I would never live a happy life again – but now I have never been happier."

"But you are still sick."

"Yes, Tom, I am a little but I do not dwell on that. I stay focused on climbing higher. One should never look back on life with regret. You gain nothing from it. It saps your energy and makes you sad. You must always look ahead and focus on climbing the next branch."

At that instant I thought of my own father and what I would do if he ever fell ill and lost his energy. My thoughts then shifted to the old man's daughter, Penny and how helpless she must have felt.

"Being sick must have made Penny very sad. Was there anything she could have done to help you get better?"

"You are a very thoughtful and compassionate boy, Tom. I wish it were that simple. The Tree of Health is one that we must climb for ourselves. When I lay in that hospital bed, there was nothing that my family could do except to sit with me, in frustration, and hold my hand. That is the heartbreak that comes from neglecting your health. The misery that you bring is not only to yourself but also to your family who are helpless as they watch you suffer."

I started imagining how I would feel if it was my own father lying there in that same hospital bed. It would be very difficult to just sit there, unable to do anything. I would be devastated if he was so sick that he could not come home to be with us.

All these thoughts made my heart sad and I looked down. The silence filled the air as I noticed a solitary ant crawling aimlessly on my shoelaces. I knew that the old man's story was not meant to upset me, but rather to remind me of the importance of the Tree of Health. I sat up and swallowed hard to get the lump out of my throat. He too sat straighter and cheerfully said, "That's enough about my life, Tom. Let's talk about how you can avoid making the same mistakes. I am going to teach you some very important lessons about health that will help you live a long, happy and energetic life. You can share these lessons with your parents. Are you ready?"

"Yes sir," I replied.

Energy Is the Only True Measure of Good Health

"The *first lesson* you need to know about good health is to recognise what it is. I have met so many people in my travels that are trying to climb higher in life only to falter because they do not know what good health truly means. They get confused or disillusioned and go through periods of low energy where they lack the will to keep climbing."

He paused to face me and asked, "Do you think you know what good health means?"

"Does it mean to feel good and strong?"

"Yes, Tom, it's amazing how your honest and simple response is so accurate. That feeling is your *energy*. People want to be healthy but don't realise that the only true measure of good health is their energy level. How else could one measure good health? If we have constant high energy, then we are healthy. It's that simple. If we have regular periods of low energy, then we know that something is not right with our body.

"I do not know why some people make it more complicated than that. They focus on their body shape like *that* is the real measure of good health. It is like saying a car will drive very fast if it looks sleek and sporty while ignoring the motor that creates the energy of motion. The Tree of Health becomes a source of stress for such people. Eating well and exercising becomes a laborious task and the focus on appearance as a measure of good health starts to drain their *emotional* energy.

"Always remember, Tom, that we are all born with different body shapes. Our focus should not be on the way our body looks but how it *feels*. Knowing this distinction is very important because we begin to focus correctly on what gives us high energy."

I understood what the old man was trying to explain because I often heard my mother complain about the way some dresses did not fit her properly. She would get frustrated that the clothes in stores were displayed on unrealistic body shapes. I wondered if my mother would feel better about herself if she knew that good health was more about energy than appearance. I made a mental note to tell her when I returned home.

The old man continued. "Now that you know about the true measure of good health, I am going to ask you another important but simple question. What do you think unleashes your energy?"

"Is it food?" I replied with a question.

"That's what most people think, Tom. We all gain fuel from the food we eat and that supplies our energy, but it does not *release* it. We all have energy by virtue of the fact that we are living humans. We *are* energy! So when we get tired, it does not necessarily mean that our body lacks a supply of energy. It means that the energy is trapped inside of us, behind a closed door. When we know this we can start to focus on the real challenge of learning how to unlock this door. We do so by focusing not only on the physical energy from the food we eat but by looking below the surface, in our hearts and minds, where our more powerful energies lie."

He paused then added in a secretive voice, "It is the most amazing discovery you will ever make in your life, Tom."

What secret was the old man hanging onto? What other source of energy could there be?

Sensing my curiosity he added, "I will help you make this discovery. But before I do so, I need you to first understand two important rules about the three branches on this Tree of Health and how they *sustain* your energy."

First Rule of Energy

"The first is that *energy begets energy*."

"What does 'beget' mean?"

"It means that to get energy, you must *use* energy, Tom. This rule is very important to learn and remember because everything I am going to teach you about having high energy rests on the simple fact that, whatever you do in life, must stimulate and perpetuate your energy to keep it flowing. When you eat, the body uses energy but it also gains the potential for energy from the food eaten. Likewise, when you play sport or work, you may spend energy but you also stimulate it and keep it flowing."

"How do you get energy from working or exercising?" I asked. "I've heard my father say that he's tired when he gets home after work."

"That's true, Tom," he answered, "but expending your energy by engaging in daily activities is a good thing. It keeps the energy flowing," he smiled and winked.

Something in that wink told me that I would soon completely understand.

"There is something else we must do to keep that energy

flowing; something that replenishes it."

"What's that?" I asked.

"The answer lies on the branch that you fell asleep on – the third branch on this Tree of Health: the branch of relaxation. The one that most people forget to climb," he said and pointed to it.

I looked up. It seemed a long time since I had woken up on that branch. It looked big, wide and peaceful as it swayed ever so gently in the soft breeze. It hung there all by itself, well away from all the other branches.

Relaxation

"This branch is where you will spend most of your alone-time, Tom."

He paused, before continuing with a quieter voice, as if we were in a library, "You must remember that in the Tree of Health, relaxing is just as important as eating well and exercising. If you do not make time to relax, you will eventually run out of puff."

"How should I relax?"

"I don't think you have to worry too much about that, Tom. Relaxation comes naturally to you because you are a child. Most adults however have so many thoughts going through their mind that they find it difficult to unwind. For them, the best way to relax is through meditation."

"What is meditation?" I asked.

"Meditation is different for everyone. It also varies for people all around the world. For some, it is listening to calming music. For others it is as simple as sitting in a comfortable, warm and quiet spot, doing nothing and thinking of nothing stimulating."

"I do that all the time," I said. "When I get tired I just sit in my room daydreaming."

"That's right, Tom. There are many practices of meditation. You can sit and focus on how your breath moves your stomach in and out, or you can repeat a soothing word softly to yourself."

He paused then added, "But I think that I have discovered the best type of meditation."

"What is it?" I asked.

"Listening to the sounds of nature. If you pay very careful attention, you will notice nature's relaxing sounds are all around us."

The old man sat still. The noises in the meadow started to grow louder and louder. What was once a faint background noise came into clear focus. I began to hear birds, a running stream and the rustling leaves above us.

"When you pay attention to nature, you become a part of it," he whispered. "It draws you in to the Earth's natural rhythm. That's when relaxation becomes effortless. When you walk in the woods or in the park, the hand of nature will reach out to touch your heart and calm your mind. This invisible force is not a secret. It is there for us to connect with when we choose to listen."

It must have been the same hand of nature that made me fall asleep on the branch, I thought to myself.

Second Rule of Energy

"I want to now share with you the second rule about energy", he continued. "And that is, when energy begets energy the net effect must be positive."

"What does *net effect* mean?"

"It is simple arithmetic, Tom. It is the energy you *earn* minus the energy you *burn*."

"So when I eat something, that is the energy I *earn*?"

"Very good; and the energy you burn is what your body spends to digest what you eat. The net effect is what you will be left with to spend on your daily activities. If what you earn is more than what you burn, then you will have high energy.

If it is less, then you will have low energy.

"This fact should drive every decision you make when choosing food. To help you make that choice, you need only remember two rules: eat less, eat often; and eat *live* not dead food."

"That's all I need to know?"

"Yes, Tom. Eating correctly should come as naturally as relaxing. We do not need to complicate it unnecessarily. Let me explain how simple these two rules are."

Eat less, eat often

"When we eat food, our body needs to transform it into energy. This is the process of digestion. But our body uses energy to digest food. The more food it has to process, the more energy it uses. There comes a tipping point in that process where the body starts to burn more energy than it earns. That point is when we eat too much.

"When that happens, our energy is sapped because our body is busy trying to digest the excess food. Low energy in turn prevents us from engaging in many activities. And when we are inactive, our body stores the energy. It sits on the shelf unused. Eventually it goes bad. That's why some people get fat, Tom. Not only because they eat too much but because their lack of activity stops the flow of energy. Fat is nothing more than a collection of unused energy!

"So to keep our energy flowing, we must stay active. To do this, we must consume the right amount of food that does not slow us down."

It made perfect sense. I started nodding.

"Our bodies only require small meals to stay energised," he continued. "That is why we need to eat less food. When we have high energy from eating the right amount of good food and we use that energy by undertaking lots of activities, our body's energy starts to flow. And that is why we must eat often. We must keep the fuel coming to replenish our body's energy supply and keep the flow of energy going. Eating *often* is just as important as eating less, otherwise we will run out of fuel."

I knew from experience what happened to me when I did not eat enough before my soccer games. I was not only lethargic; I was grumpy. The coach always reminded us to eat good food but he never explained the importance of how much to eat and when to eat.

I asked the old man, "How often should I eat?"

"It is different for everyone, Tom. It depends on your size and how much activity you have in your day, but I can tell you that the healthiest and most active people I have come across eat regularly throughout the day."

"Is that what you do?"

"It certainly is. I eat even smaller meals throughout the day because my digestion is not as efficient as it used to be. The heart attack slowed the engine of my body. That is why I also have to make sure I eat the *right* food."

Eat live foods

"This leads me to the second rule about the branch of nutrition."

The old man paused and asked, "Are you keeping up, Tom?"

"Yes," I replied and nodded.

"Excellent. This next lesson is related to the first but is even easier to remember.

"Eat *live* foods!" he said with gusto.

"What do you mean by that?" I asked.

"It means eating produce that is as close to nature as possible. For example, if we pick an apple from a tree, that is a live food because it was living on the tree. The moment it is picked, it starts to lose its *live* energy. Therefore the absolute best time to eat an apple is soon after it is picked. That's when it gives us the most energy. The longer we leave it, the less *live* energy it retains. Therefore, the time taken for a food to come from the earth to the kitchen table is the best way to determine its liveliness.

"The other thing to note about food is that the further it is from its original form, the less energy it has. The moment you take an apple and bake it into a pie, it loses its live energy. This rule applies to all the food we eat. The more processed it is, the more dead it becomes. A fresh baked potato has much more *live* energy than a packet of chips. Grain that is freshly milled and unprocessed makes the best bread. So if ever you find yourself hungry for a snack, open the fridge and not the pantry. That is where you will find live foods.

"We are *alive*, Tom, why would we ever eat *dead* food? Processed food, no matter its original form, is dead. The moment you cook, package and store it, the energy in it starts to rapidly die. When eaten, it produces a negative net effect because it is harder for the body to digest. Our stomach has to sift through the dead part of the food to find the living part and this wastes precious energy.

"That's why it is very important for you to eat live foods. They give you the most energy and take the least effort for the body to process. You will *earn* more energy than you *burn*," he concluded with a smile and a wink.

I always thought of good nutrition as something a lot more complicated than just eating live foods. I admired the athletes I saw on television and often wondered whether they took some special supplements to make them so energetic; I assumed they did. At least that's what my mother told me, to get me to take my vitamins every morning.

"My mother gives me vitamins to take," I said. "She says that they will give me energy."

"When you eat live foods you do not need to take vitamins,"

he quickly responded.

The old man stood up and started walking away. He turned and briefly added, "Oh and the other thing to remember is to eat fruit and vegetables that are *in season*. Our bodies need different nutrients at different times of the year."

He then beckoned me to follow him. "Come, Tom. Come with me, I want to show you something truly amazing. I want to show you how to tap into a source of immense energy."

Our True Source of Energy

The old man walked a little farther from the Tree of Health and turned to look at it. I did the same and instinctively looked up thinking that he was going to talk more about its three branches. Instead I noticed that he was looking down at the base of the tree.

I looked to the ground momentarily and back at him, puzzled.

"Look carefully," he prompted.

I again looked down and this time noticed what looked like woody branches meandering above and beneath the surface of the ground.

"Oh, branches."

"They are not branches, Tom. They are roots," he replied as he knelt down and swept some of the leaves from the ground with his hands. He revealed an intricate network of roots.

"Each Tree of Life in the circle is connected to the Tree of Health below the ground," he said.

He pointed to the tree behind him and added, "These roots come from the Tree of Love."

He walked over to the next tree in the circle, knelt down and wiped the ground cover to reveal more roots. "These come from the Tree of Family."

He stood up and added, "All these seven Trees support the Tree of Health by strengthening its roots."

"How could that be?" I asked. "It looks like the Tree of Health supports them."

"The Tree of Health may support the seven others *above* the ground through its branches but they support it *beneath* the ground."

He paused.

"This is the *true* source of our energy, Tom," he added with a wise lift of his eyebrows.

The old man looked at me like he had just revealed the most amazing secret in the world.

"Our *physical* energy may come from the branches on the Tree of Health but the seven other Trees support our health by supplying three invisible and more powerful energies. It is these three other energies that either release or deplete our physical energy."

I paid very careful attention. The enthusiasm in his voice got me excited. It sounded like he was leading to something extraordinary.

"I want to show you something," he continued. "Something that will help you appreciate the importance of these three other energies."

He put his hand into his right pocket and pulled out a small metal object.

"Is that a compass?"

"Yes, Tom."

He placed the compass on the open palm of his left hand. It was about the size of a chestnut with metal sides and a glass top cover. Inside there was a small metal hand with two points. The letters 'N.S.E.W.' were inscribed for each quadrant.

He then said, "Imagine for a minute that this is not a magnetic compass but your energy compass. You can call it the P.I.E.S. compass. So instead of North, South, East and West, it represents your four energies. 'P' stands for Physical, 'I' for Intellectual,

'E' for Emotional and 'S' for Spiritual.

"*Physical* energy is what your body displays when it is active and in motion. *Intellectual* energy is your mind's energy. It is the thinking that precedes your actions. *Emotional* energy is how you *feel* about what happens in life. *Spiritual* energy is the love, compassion and connection you have for all living things on this Earth, especially people.

"The important rule to remember about these four energies is that they must all be balanced. Your physical energy will not be high if one of the other energies is low.

"If your thinking is not positive, you will end up focusing on fruitless pursuits that give you little in the way of purpose and direction. If your feelings are hurt or filled with the negative emotions of anger or fear, it will dampen your hearts passion and courage. If you are not satisfying your spiritual need, you will not be able to tap into the force of life on this Earth. How you *think* and *feel* affects your body, Tom. It affects your physical energy.

"That is why you must focus on all four energies. When they are perfectly balanced you will experience life with unlimited energy."

The old man looked at me with kind eyes and said, "I want you to have this compass. It will remind you of your P.I.E.S. energy and will guide you whenever you are lost in the realms of lethargy and apathy."

"Thank you sir," I replied. I felt very special that he was giving me the compass for keeps. I could not wait to show it to my family as evidence of my time with the old man.

I looked at it again, examining the four quadrants. I knew from my time in Boy Scouts that to navigate accurately, the metal hand in the compass must be balanced.

"How do I balance these four energies?" I asked.

"When you live a complete life in these Trees of Love,

Family, Work, Friendship, Learning, Wealth and Charity you automatically achieve balance. But if you neglect even one of these areas of life, your energy will drop by that one. If you neglect more, you will lose even more energy. And if you neglect them all, your flow of energy will cease altogether. That's why some people lose their physical energy for a long time. Not because their body has failed them, but because they have failed their body by not filling their life with purposeful activities that engage their heart and mind.

"If ever you experience such periods, Tom, you should not only climb the three branches on your Tree of Health, you should also take stock of your life to ensure that the source of your three other energies are flowing from the seven other Trees of Life. It is this focus that will keep you climbing. Your energy will follow you as you climb higher."

The Heart and Mind

He turned to face me and added, "Ultimately, Tom, the real power is in your heart and mind. The secret to unleashing your physical energy is to develop a partnership between the two."

He paused to consider and added, "But the climb higher always begins in the mind, because positive thoughts leads to positive feelings. Where your mind goes, your heart is sure to follow. What your mind focuses on grows and grows; your heart has no choice but to follow that lead. Therefore, if you learn how to control your mind, you will be able to balance all four of your energies.

"I can tell that you are a boy who lives from the heart, and that is a good thing. But as you grow older you have to learn how to control your mind so it leads your heart in the right direction."

"How do I do that?" I asked, sensing that this was a very important lesson.

"By following a positive pattern of thinking," he said, again with a wise lift of his eyebrows.

"Is that the pattern of thinking you taught Simon the actor?"

"It sure is, Tom. If you *focus on your goals and dreams*, your passion will awaken and direct your energy. If you take *action with courage*, your energy will rise to the surface and manifest itself. If you are *motivated by love* in everything you do, you will enrich your heart's emotional and spiritual energy. If you wholeheartedly *accept* the winds of change that blow your way, you will learn its lessons and embrace its opportunities. If you are *grateful* for what you have, you will not waste energy focusing on what you don't have. If you are *giving* of your time and wealth to others, your energy will multiply. If you are *fearless and adventurous* in life, you will perpetuate the energy you get from discovering new goals and dreams."

He paused to take a breath.

"In this Tree of Health, I taught you how to sustain and unleash your physical energy. Let me now teach you how to control your mind's energy. Your thoughts, Tom!"

At the time, I never fully appreciated what the wise old man was sharing with me. As I grew older however, I realised he had been leading me on a journey – a voyage to harness the power of my mind. The eight Trees of Life was my road map and the Circle of Conscious Living became my guide.

Part Two

THE CIRCLE OF CONSCIOUS LIVING

CHAPTER 11

The Circle of Conscious Living

"To enjoy good health, to bring true
happiness to one's family, to bring peace to all,
one must first discipline and control one's own
mind. If a man can control his mind ... all
wisdom and virtue will naturally come to him."

Buddha

*We often underestimate the ability of children to
understand life's wisdom. The world may appear to be
complex but the fundamentals of living are really very simple.
Children understand this more than adults because daily issues
like finances and work deadlines do not distract them. Children
also do not live with arrogance, pride or self-importance. So
they are open to learning much easier than adults.*

*Had I met the wise old man when I was older, I may have
better understood the guiding principles in the eight Trees and
the importance of climbing higher in each of them, but I may
not have taken action. As adults we often dismiss life's little
lessons as too childish for the real world. But I have learned
and witnessed that the most successful people in the world focus
relentlessly on the fundamentals of living. They eat well. They*

exercise. They love. They laugh. They learn. They innovate. They create. They inspire. They share.

Conversely I have met cynical people who view life as a complex maze. They think that success is either inherited or happens by luck. Their cynical mind is not easily guided by simple truths. It does not dream. It does not motivate action. It becomes weak with indecision and eventually causes stagnation.

I look back on my time with the old man and cannot help but feel grateful that I met him when I was only eight years old. It meant that I wholeheartedly accepted the guiding wisdom in the eight Trees without any cynicism whatsoever. I focused on and got to climb each Tree of Life. I heeded his advice by not neglecting any. I pursued my passions and disciplined myself to climb daily. Sometimes it brought me hardship, but I never stopped climbing.

That much was easy.

The most challenging part, however, came in the way I climbed. For it is one thing to know where you are going in life but another to know how to get there. In my adult years, I realised more and more that my eight Trees were merely a guide, albeit a powerful one. They directed me to what I should be climbing, but they did not teach me how to climb.

There came a time when I became disillusioned with my achievements. I felt like they were not so great if it meant having to be selfish, and even ruthless, to get what I wanted out of life. My adult-induced cynicism grew and I started doubting the wisdom. For a time, I lost focus and stopped climbing altogether. The fruit sat on the branches uneaten and eventually fell to the ground, wasted. I became unhappy.

It was during this particularly difficult period in my life when I realised that though my climb had been adventurous and taken me to significant heights, something was still lacking. That for all these years I had forgotten the second and most *important wisdom the old man had taught me. It was hidden in my subconscious, only to be unlocked by the most challenging phase of my life.*

It was on one particular night, at my lowest moment, when I awoke in the early hours of the morning with my heart beating seemingly out of my chest. I sat up in bed, sweating profusely. The storm raging inside my heart subsided a little and I decided to go for a walk to calm myself and gain some perspective. Before I left the house, I went into the attic and dug up an old journal with many blank pages left in it. It was one that I stopped writing in and had tossed aside like an unwanted buddy. It felt good to blow the dust off it. A new beginning? Perhaps.

I left the house and after a short walk, arrived at a serene spot overlooking a nearby lake where I sat waiting for the sunrise. I turned my attention to the journal in the hope of writing something, anything! I closed my eyes and tried to remember the old man's face and the sound of his voice. Our time together seemed so long ago.

As my hopes for inspiration started to fade, I felt a bright light suddenly fall on my face. The warmth of it tickled my cheeks. I opened my eyes in surprise only to see that it was the sun greeting me like an old friend.

It was in that instant that a series of memories came flooding back; memories of my time with the old man during the second half of that fortuitous day in the meadow. I closed my eyes again and remembered that it was the afternoon when he shared with me the most powerful way to control my thoughts.

As I recalled the wisdom and the lessons, I began to write profusely in my journal. I wrote and wrote until my hand ached. I smiled as I wrote. I felt like I was eight years of age again. I felt empowered. It was like something inside of me had awakened to see the truth. The truth was that although I had been climbing higher in life, I had not been doing so with a conscious mind and a congruent heart.

This truth opened the door to the next phase of my life – the door to intellectual and emotional enlightenment. It was the second piece of the puzzle that had been missing and I had found it in the sunrise.

The old man taught me the simplest of ways to develop a strong mind. He taught me a pattern of thinking that was impenetrable to the chaos and negativity of the outside world. It armed me with the wisdom that would strengthen my mind and my heart forever.

He taught me the Circle of Conscious Living.

A New Pattern of Thinking

The day seemed to be standing still in time. I sat there in a happy daze looking around the meadow of lush green grass. I looked up at the clear blue sky and noticed one small cloud drifting by. The sun was shining above the eight Trees and I could feel a gentle coastal breeze beginning to blow softly on my face.

The old man had just finished relating his life stories, including his many mistakes. I learned about all stages of his life, each teaching me a valuable lesson. I felt like I knew him better than I knew myself. We had only been talking for a few hours and yet it seemed like I had known him my whole life.

He left to go to the nearby stream to fetch some more water for both of us. As I waited, I lay back on the grass imagining how my life would be as an adult. I tried to imagine what I would achieve in each of my eight Trees. A sense of excitement filled my body and butterflies in my stomach started to dance.

As I contemplated my future I also started imagining some terrible things that could go wrong; circumstances that would stop me from climbing. What if some of the boys started bullying me at school? What if I got sick? What if my parents died? What if? What if? All the 'what ifs' popped into my head and my heart started pounding with fear. I opened my eyes to bring me back to the present, sat up and noticed the old man walking back towards me. He spoke as he approached. "Remember, Tom, that life will not always be rosy. Even if you do climb all these eight Trees, life will still bring you challenges."

He arrived and sat on the grass next to me and added, "Some people are tested more than others. It could be illness or loss of a loved one or losing your job. Or even living in a country that suffers a natural disaster or war. We cannot control such random events. The best that we can do is to keep climbing."

"But I started imagining some horrible things that could go wrong," I said anxiously.

"Dear Tom, I can see that you are upset by the pattern of negative thinking you talked yourself into."

"I don't understand," I interjected, "I didn't say anything to myself. These bad thoughts just popped into my head."

"We talk to ourselves all the time," he responded. "We do it so instinctively that we do not even realise that it is an internal conversation we are having. But the good news is that just as you can talk yourself into a negative pattern of thinking, you can also talk yourself into a positive one.

"There are some people who get defeated by life's setbacks and lose their will to climb. That is a choice they make because they view their challenges negatively. They blame others for their problems or they blame their circumstances or even themselves. They tell themselves, 'I can never do that because I was not taught to' or 'I don't live in the right neighbourhood or go to the right school' or 'I am not strong enough or smart enough' or 'I might get hurt' or – my personal favourite – 'I don't have time!'

"When someone *thinks* like this, they are talking themselves out of climbing higher in life. The reality is, no one is ever born into a perfect set of circumstances. And, the other reality is that we all have the same time. So the difference between us can only be our state of mind.

"I have now realised that the only thing we can control is *how* we think and *what* we think. This is very important because thinking is what precedes the decisions we make and the actions we take. If we think the wrong way we will make poor decisions in life. It's as simple as that.

"I used to talk myself out of a lot of things *because* of my unconscious negative thinking."

He paused, as he often did, before revealing one of his thought-provoking lessons. But this time, the serious look in his eyes told me that this lesson was very important.

"But *one day* I discovered a new pattern of thinking that changed all that," he added.

The Circle of Conscious Living

"I want to share with you the most powerful way to manage your thinking, Tom. It will make you strong and fearless. Would you like to hear it?"

"Yes please."

My curiosity was sparked.

"Where did you discover this pattern of thinking?" I asked.

"When I lay in that hospital bed recovering from my heart attack, I had a lot of time on my hands. I reflected on all the poor choices I made and realised that there are no mistakes in life, only lessons. And I was lucky enough to learn a life-changing one.

"I learned that you could train your mind to follow a conscious pattern of thinking that always leads to a happy outlook; one that can reverse and flip any negative thoughts. I call it the

Circle of Conscious Living," he said thoughtfully.

"There are some challenges that you will face throughout your life, Tom. Most will be outside of your control. It happens to all of us. But how you process and *think* about such challenges is the key to life-long happiness."

"So how am I supposed to think?" I asked.

"You must learn to *consciously* follow a positive pattern of thinking. Whatever happens in your day, whether it's good or bad, can be processed using this pattern. It will make your mind strong and your heart even stronger."

The old man put his right hand into the pocket of his long garment. He pulled out a small scroll with a string around it. He untied and unrolled the linen-like paper.

"I want you to have this," he said. "This is the five step pattern to the Circle of Conscious Living. Since leaving the hospital, I have been living by this Circle. It is the most powerful way to think. It will give your mind the discipline it needs for you to keep climbing higher and will help you climb back up if ever you fall off and lose your way in life."

He handed me the scroll. I placed it on the ground next to me and unrolled it. I found four little pebbles and placed them on top, one for each corner, to keep it open. I studied each step in the Circle briefly and then looked up at the old man, only to find his face beaming with a proud smile. It seemed like he had been waiting a long time to share this with someone.

CHAPTER 12

STEP ONE:
Focus on Your Goals and Dreams

"A good head and a good heart are always a formidable combination."

Nelson Mandela

I looked down at the scroll and focused on the first step in the Circle. I looked back over to the old man and saw that he was sketching something on the ground with a stick. While he drew, he said, "The first step in the Circle of Conscious Living is the beginning of a new partnership between your heart and mind, Tom. It is the start and finish to the Circle."

"What are you drawing?" I asked.

"It's a heart inside a mind; because this step is all about your thoughts and feelings," he responded and continued focusing.

He finished sketching, looked back at me and added, "This is the most important step in the Circle because it interrupts and breaks old and destructive patterns of thinking. It is the point where old momentum is halted and a new series of thoughts and feelings are triggered in the right direction. Without this first step, the next four steps in the Circle will be directionless.

"You see, Tom, our thoughts and feelings are like a stack of dominos. We can set them up in such a way so they follow the path we want them to take. The way to set them up and the path they take depend on what goals our mind focuses on and what dreams our heart yearns for. That's why this is the first step in the Circle."

I understood what goals were. My mother had taught me to write my goals down for each of my subjects at school. My father had taught me to have goals when training for soccer. I did not understand, though, how goals could be different to dreams.

"What is the difference between goals and dreams?" I asked.

"Dreams live in our hearts whereas goals are formed in our minds," he answered and paused to make sure I comprehended the difference.

Our Dreams

"Dreams give us the motivation to want to achieve our goals," he continued. "They ignite a very powerful force that lives inside all of us. This force makes us want to jump in the air with excitement and drives us to overcome any obstacles that stand in the way of our goals.

"That force is *passion*, Tom. And it only comes out to play when we visualise living a great life in each of these eight Trees."

"Visualise? Do you mean imagine?" I asked.

"Yes, Tom. It is about imagining your best dreams."

I looked up at the Trees to imagine what my life would be like as an adult in each of them.

"Would you like me to teach you how to visualise?" He asked.

"Yes, please."

"Okay I want you to close your eyes and think of the eight Trees above you."

I closed my eyes and sensed their presence.

"Now I want you to imagine climbing one of them," he directed.

The Tree of Learning shone brighter in my mind. I wanted to open my eyes to see if it was in fact brighter, but the old man must have seen my eyelids flicker and said, "It is important that you keep your eyes closed, Tom. The imagination is greater that way.

"Now tell me, which Tree are you visualising?"

"The Tree of Learning," I responded.

"Very good. Now tell me what you imagine happening?"

"I see myself in class paying close attention to my teacher, Miss Smith. She is writing something on the board and asks me to read an excerpt from a book. Some of the boys at the back of the class are making fun of me, calling me the teacher's pet."

The old man interrupted, "I need you to remember one important thing when you visualise your dreams. You should never let anyone mock you for having them. They are your own personal fairytale. So you can imagine what you want with pure abandon."

I closed my eyes again and this time lost myself in my heart's feelings. I forgot all sense of time and started talking quickly and excitedly in a way I had never done before.

"I see myself at the front of the class reading while the teacher and students listen. I am standing tall and reading with a confident voice. After I finish, my teacher congratulates me, and the students clap.

"I see myself reading stories about adventure at home and sharing my ideas in class the next day. I see the teacher telling me how pleased she is. I see myself in the library, scouring the shelves, looking for more books on adventure. I also see myself writing stories of my own and sharing them in class.

"I see myself receiving an award from the principal for my contribution. I see myself at home with my mum and dad, talking about my award and reading to them some of the short stories that I have written. I am speaking with enthusiasm and my parents are listening to every word I say, without distraction."

I paused to take a breath. I kept my eyes closed and realised that my face must have been beaming with a big smile. It felt like it was tingling with excitement. I was amazed at what I had just visualised. And I suddenly felt a sense of urgency to go to school and make my dream happen.

The old man then explained, "You see, Tom, once we dream our best life in any one of these Trees, our passion is ignited and we are stirred into action. That's when our mind kicks-in and formulates the goals we have to achieve. Our goals come flowing quickly once we dream a wonderful vision of our life in any one of these eight Trees. Once we commit ourselves to that dream in our heart, our goals are never forgotten because they become etched in our mind."

At that instant, a flock of ducks flew overhead, quacking noisily. Without looking, the old man pointed upwards and said, "Those ducks get it. They instinctively know when and where they are migrating. They do not need to write anything down. We are no different to them. When we consciously focus on our goals, our mind will instinctively tell us where to go and what to do.

"Now, I want you to continue telling me your dreams in the Tree of Learning. What is it that you truly love and would like to learn more about? I do not mean topics that you are taught at school. I want to know what you are curious about in life."

I closed my eyes again and continued, "I love to learn about nature and how the Earth works. I love learning about weather patterns so I can predict when it will rain or storm. I see myself studying cloud formations in all parts of the world, but especially near my hometown. I want to chase storms to learn how they form and move. I want to write about my adventures. I see myself in class, teaching about storms and cyclones. The students are engaged in what I have to say. I show them pictures of storms that I have chased. I love sharing my experiences with them."

As I spoke those last few words, my smile grew even bigger. I realised in that moment that I wanted to be a *teacher*. This realisation was overwhelming, as I felt my body fill with energy and excitement. I opened my eyes and met those of the old man smiling back at me.

"I want to be a teacher!" I said enthusiastically.

"It seems to me, Tom, that you are a teacher at heart," he replied with a knowing smile. "Your heart is telling your mind what it must focus on. You love to teach, and in particular, you love adventure and the study of nature. Now that your heart has discovered that dream, every day your mind will seek out the goals you need to achieve to make that dream a reality."

The old man paused to search my thoughts.

"What's the matter, Tom? You seem a little quiet."

"I'm fine," I responded. "It's just that nobody has ever taught me this before. You make it so simple."

He sensed my gratitude, looked at me humbly and simply said, "Thank you."

Our Goals

After a brief silence, I asked, "What goals do I have to achieve to become a great teacher?"

"Ultimately, Tom, your goal is to be educated to qualify you to teach. You have to finish school and probably go to university to learn more about what you want to teach and how to teach effectively. But before you reach that goal you can set yourself many smaller goals to help you get there. You can start by borrowing books from the library about teaching. You can join or start your own discussion groups. You can also ask your favourite teachers to share their tips on teaching. Your journey of discovery will take you in so many directions. Most importantly, you will be doing what you love."

The more I thought about teaching, the more I liked the idea. I closed my eyes again and visualised standing in front of a class of students. I started to smile and felt my heart expanding with excitement. I also visualised myself teaching family and friends. But this time the vision was not only of me talking about meteorology, but teaching about life and the eight Trees.

The old man interrupted my daydream.

"I just taught you how to visualise your dreams and hold them in your heart; now I want to teach you how to make your dreams a reality. This is where goals come in. They help your mind focus on what you want. And, when you focus daily on what you want, you start to lose interest in the things that do not matter.

"So, I want to share with you six lessons that will help you set the right goals. These lessons are very important, Tom, because unless you know how to manage your goals, your dreams will remain fanciful."

1. Have a complete set of goals

"The first lesson is that, to live a complete life you must have a complete set of goals."

"What do you mean by that?" I asked.

"Well, you just figured out what your goals are in the Tree of Work and Tree of Learning. Can you now tell me what your goals are for all the other areas of life?"

I looked up at the sparkling sun-lit trees for inspiration.

"That's right, Tom. Your goals can be found in these eight

Trees. Life will not be complete unless you have goals in each of them. Most people strive for a balanced life, but don't realise that balance only comes when you have a complete set of goals.

"Some people think that the only worthy goals are material ones. They aim for items to buy. They may strive to buy a new car, a house in a particular area, or any number of material items. They ignore the more obvious goals like being a thoughtful partner in the Tree of Love or living with high energy in the Tree of Health.

"Some people even set the wrong goals. I know this because, in the Tree of Work, I used to set goals for myself that were misguided. My goals often related to my getting promotions and pay rises instead of creating and achieving something worthwhile at work.

"*Your* goals, Tom, must be true to the wisdom I have shared with you in each of these eight Trees. That's why I shared them with you first, so you would understand this first step in the circle of Conscious Living and know exactly what goals to focus on and climb for in life."

2. Own your own goals

"How do I know what *my* goals are?" I asked.

"The answer to that question leads me to the second lesson – you must own your own goals. Nobody can tell you what they are. You have to figure them out for yourself. Each of these Trees was planted when you were born, so they are unique to you. Therefore your goals are uniquely yours.

"There are however common goals that we all share on the highest branches in these eight Trees of Life. Would you like to know what they are?"

"Yes please."

He looked up and started to recount as he pointed to

each tree.

"On the Tree of Health, it is to have a body that is strong, energetic and relaxed.

"On the Tree of Love, it is to love yourself and a partner who loves you equally in return.

"On the Tree of Family, it is to be a part of a family that cares and supports one another.

"On the Tree of Work, it is innovation and achievement in the humble service of others.

"On the Tree of Friendship, it is fun and laughter.

"On the Tree of Learning, it is knowledge and creativity.

"On the Tree of Wealth, it is freedom.

"On the Tree of Charity, it is empathy, compassion and sharing.

"These are the fruits on the highest branches that we *all* must savour in life. Our own specific goals must be aligned to these end goals."

"Can you please give me some examples of specific goals?" I asked.

"Certainly, Tom. I can you give some specific goals for the Tree of Health. In fact I will tell you some of my own. On the branch of exercise one of my goals is to be able to walk eight kilometres every day. My other goal is to do fifty push-ups in one go. I practice daily for both these goals. I am getting closer and closer to achieving them. Every day I find myself getting stronger. And once I do achieve them, do you know what I'm going to do? I'm going to set myself new goals.

"Which leads me to the third lesson."

3. Always set new goals

"Always remember that while you may be reaching for what you think is the highest branch, your Trees of Life will continue to grow new branches for you to climb. If you don't climb them, those areas of your life will stop growing. And that's when you start living a small life. You don't want to do that, Tom. You want to live a fulfilling life, with satisfying goals. That's why you need to constantly set new goals, no matter how high you climb.

"Sometimes your goals and dreams may change, and that is okay. You may climb a branch that yields little fruit. You will need to try something else. So, go ahead and change branches. There is no problem altering your direction in life, as long as you keep moving and setting new goals for yourself."

"How do I do that?" I asked.

"I will give you an example. You mentioned earlier that you'd like to earn and save your own money."

"Yes, I'd like to save enough for a bike. I deposit coins in my piggy bank every time Dad arrives from work and hands me some loose change. Dad also gives me money for doing chores around the house."

"Let me then ask you this, are you going to stop saving money once you have bought the bike?"

"Probably not," I replied.

"That's right. Once you reach that goal you may set yourself another target, of say, saving one hundred dollars. And once you reach that you may even start to save one thousand dollars, and so on. That is the essence of climbing higher. You never stop setting new goals. There is always a higher branch to reach for.

"Once you reach step five in the Circle of Conscious Living, you will see how easy it is to keep dreaming bigger things and setting new goals."

I looked down at the scroll and to step five in the Circle. It read: 'Be Fearless and Adventurous'. I liked the idea of being fearless.

4. Associate with people who have common goals

The old man next said, "Do you remember the story I told you about the amazing friendship I developed with a work colleague and the goals we achieved together?"

"Yes, I remember. It was the one about integrity."

"Very good, Tom. Well that story also serves as an example of what can happen when two or more people go after the same goal. Their combined effort makes it easier to achieve that goal because they will inspire and motivate one another. The energy between them multiplies and moves them towards their goal a lot faster."

"Is it like pushing a go-cart up a hill?" I asked. "Will the goal to reach the top happen a lot faster if you have someone helping?"

"That's exactly what it's like. When we push a cart up a hill on our own, we are more likely to give up when we get tired and lose motivation. Having a friend motivates us to never give up.

"It is truly amazing to witness a team striving to reach the same goal. Their hearts and minds appear to be synchronized. Such a positive alliance only happens occasionally in life. When it does, you should not take it for granted. You must embrace it!"

5. Pay attention to your energy levels

The old man paused to collect his thoughts.

"Tom, do you remember what I said about the Tree of Health and your energy level? I said that if you are *not* living a complete life, your energy will be low – even if you eat well, exercise and relax. Well, the fifth lesson is to always pay close attention to your energy level. It is an excellent indicator of how big your goals are. The bigger your goals, the bigger your energy. It's as simple as that. And when you have *really* big goals in all eight areas of your life, you will experience an energy explosion! You will bounce out of bed every morning.

"So you should never ignore that message from your body. Bring your awareness to it. The best way to do that is to write in a journal every day."

"A Journal?"

6. Keep a journal

"Yes, Tom. That leads me to the sixth and most important lesson. Keeping a journal will help you manage your goals and keep track of the actions you need to take to achieve them. It empowers you to become your own guide and teacher."

I liked the idea of becoming my own teacher. I wanted to be wise just like the old man.

"I want to give you something," he said. "Something that will help you immeasurably in life."

He reached into the pocket of his garment that seemed to have an endless store of interesting things, and pulled out a brown leather journal. An image on the cover reflected the sunlight. As he steadied it in his hands, I noticed the outline of a tree etched in shiny gold leaf. It looked mystical, like something from an Indiana Jones movie.

"This is a unique journal," he said. "I use it to write about my thoughts and feelings each and every day; in times of celebration and in times of trouble. I use it to apply the five steps in the Circle of Conscious Living to each area of my life. Writing in it daily is critical to maintaining my focus."

The old man extended his hand to show me the journal.

"Writing in this journal is no different to eating healthy food to sustain your body. This journal will sustain your heart and mind. It keeps your heart and mind focused on the things that matter."

He fanned the pages and left it open. I noticed that the left page was lined whereas the right page was blank.

"The left page is your *action* page, Tom," he said. "It is what you have to *do* for the day. The right page is your *reflection* page, where you write about how you *felt* about your day.

"The left page is for your head and the right page is for your heart."

He paused to make sure I understood.

"I have a school diary," I said, "but I guess that's different."

"This journal is more than about school. It is about life. Therefore you should use it to write about your daily achievements in all eight areas, including school."

"When should I write in it?" I asked.

"The best time to write on the *action* page is at the end of each day. You write about what action you need to take for the next day. It is good to get things out of your head and into your journal while it is fresh in your mind. Otherwise, you will toss and turn at night with thoughts that go round and round in your head."

"What about the *reflection* page?"

"You should write on this page when you wake each morning.

"For as long as man has walked this Earth, sunrise has been the best time for reflection and taking stock of one's feelings. It is the time of day when you can properly judge the truth to your feelings.

"Journaling your feelings will set you up for a happy day, Tom. It will strengthen your heart and make every action you take during the day decisive and certain."

The old man extended both his hands, this time to give me the journal. "I want you to have this," he said. "It is my gift to you."

I was a little shy to be receiving a present from someone I had only just met. But he looked at me with that same kind face that greeted me when I first woke up in the meadow.

I reached out to receive the journal and gripped it tight. I felt a tingling sensation up my spine and goose bumps tickled my arms. I knew that receiving the journal would be the beginning of a long friendship – a friendship with myself.

There was silence and I figured that he was waiting for me to open it. So I fanned the pages with my thumb until it opened on a random page. I looked closer and noticed the outline of eight trees. The following words were written across the top of each tree: *'Health – Love – Family – Friendship – Learning – Work – Wealth – Charity'*.

The old man finally said, "This journal will help you keep track of where you are spending your time. At the end of each week, on a Sunday night, you should review which areas of your life you have climbed and written about. It will help you take stock of where your attention has been focused. You will also notice which Trees you are neglecting.

"*That* is the key feature of this journal, Tom. Your eight Trees are your guides and this journal is an account of your commitment to living a complete life in each of them. If, by the end of the week, you have not written about one Tree, then you will know that you are not being true to your commitment. And you will realise that your life is not complete. That's when you must take action, and bring your attention back on the Trees you are neglecting. That's why this journal is the most powerful tool you will ever have. It will help you stay focused on your goals and dreams."

CHAPTER 13

STEP TWO:
Take Action with Courage
Yet Be Motivated by Love

*"A little knowledge that acts
is worth infinitely more than
knowledge that is idle."*

Kahlil Gibran

*T*he knowledge I gained from the wise old man about goals
and dreams awakened the passion in my heart. My mind
was likewise filled with many possibilities. I was excited because
I knew that all I had to do was visualise my best life in the eight
Trees to discover my goals in each of them. I also felt a sense of
restlessness and the urge to start taking action.

It was at that moment that the old man started teaching me
the second step in the Circle of Conscious Living.

He taught me that having goals and dreams without taking
action creates an illusion, which is a way of lying to yourself.
And when you lie to yourself, you start to lose trust in your
abilities. Eventually this vicious circle of wishing and dreaming
followed by inaction leads to regret. And regret is most painful

when you know what to do in life but choose not to do it.

He showed me the way to action by teaching me to have courage. He did this by relating to the most unlikely of earthly creatures.

The Wisdom of the Turtle

As the old man and I sat under the Tree of Friendship, we both looked to our right to notice a turtle plodding along. We could see that the path was worn from its previous journeys to the sea.

The old man gestured towards the turtle and said, "We can learn four very important lessons from the humble turtle, Tom."

At that very instant, the turtle craned its neck in our direction. It looked like it was smiling at us. I turned to tell the old man and noticed a similar smile on his face. It seemed that he and the turtle shared a common wisdom. The turtle then returned its focus back to the path and kept moving.

The old man turned to me and said, "To help you remember the second step in the Circle of Conscious Living, I want you to think of the turtle."

The Turtle's First Lesson - *Take daily steps in the direction of your goals and dreams*

"The first lesson I want you to learn from the turtle is that small steps in the right direction will always get you there."

"But the turtle is so slow," I laughed.

"That may be so but the turtle does not stop until it reaches its destination. That is what you must also do in life, Tom. You must take daily action no matter how small. And you must plan your action by writing it in the journal I gave you, otherwise you may not head in the right direction."

I gazed out into the meadow to see where the turtle was up to in its journey, and to my amazement it was out of sight. Small steps really do add up, I thought.

The old man noticed where my attention was. He pointed in the direction of the turtle and said, "The combination of focusing on your goals and taking small daily steps is the quickest and straightest path to your dreams, Tom. The results will surprise you."

The Turtle's Second Lesson - *Courage*

I was eager to hear what else I could possibly learn from the turtle. So I said, "I have read the story of the tortoise and the hare and I understand that the tortoise made it to the finish line faster because it did not get distracted. Can the turtle teach us more than that?"

"The story of the tortoise and the hare is not just about focusing on goals," he replied. "It is not just about how the hasty hare kept getting distracted. It is also a story about the turtles *courage*."

I could not imagine what the turtle could possibly teach me about courage. When it came to courage, I always thought of majestic animals like lions and eagles.

But the old man surprised me.

"The turtle is slow and therefore an easy target for predators. It relies on its strong outer shell to protect it. But herein lies its dilemma. The turtle cannot move towards its goal of reaching the sea unless it comes out of its shell to expose itself. It physically cannot move forward until it sticks its neck out.

"There's a lesson in that for us. We must likewise stick our neck out to move towards our goals. It takes courage to do that. We must go outside our comfort zone. We must not let fear keep us in our own shell. We must think of the turtle and remind ourselves that in life's travels courage must drive, not fear."

Fear

"Fear prevents us from climbing higher. Fear of rejection keeps us from making new friends. Fear of ridicule keeps us from learning and expressing new ideas. Fear of getting hurt keeps us from finding love. Fear of failure keeps us from trying new ideas at work. Fear keeps us from living our best life!

"Fear comes to us when we step outside our comfort zone and into the unknown. We fear because we do not know what will happen to us in this unchartered territory. More often than not we fear terrible events that are unlikely to ever happen.

"But do you know what, Tom? Fear is also an opportunity for us to display our courage. Everyone feels fear. The turtle feels fear when it comes out of its shell; but it still does so because it knows that it is the only way to reach its destination. It has the courage to stick its neck out, despite the fear.

"And do you know something else about fear? It is a testament to our amazing imagination. It actually takes a creative mind to conjure up fear. The more vivid our imagination, the more we can envisage what could go wrong. So when we feel fear, we should be grateful for having such creativity."

"Really?"

"Yes, Tom, but let me first ask you this. You love to play soccer don't you?"

"Yes, it's my favourite sport." I wasn't sure how he knew that. Had I mentioned it?

"Well then, if you could choose between the imagined fear of hurting yourself in soccer, or the imagined bliss of scoring a sensational goal, which one would you choose?"

"Scoring a goal, of course!" I replied excitedly, as I visualised what it would feel like.

"Then, why not use your imagination to push passed your fear. Choose to visualise your best dreams not your worst nightmares. Focus your imagination on what you want rather than what you don't want."

"It is difficult sometimes," I said, "when I go onto the soccer field. I fear getting hurt, especially when we play a team with really big players. I get scared to compete for the ball. Or I fear that my teammates will mock me if I miss an easy shot at goal. On those days, I make sure I do not try too hard to get to the ball."

After I uttered those last few words, I fell silent and looked down, knowing how disappointing that must have sounded. I realised that I was not being courageous. I was living in my shell.

The old man noticed my dismay and said, "You have just realised your lesson, Tom. You have used your imagination in the past to stop you from playing your best game. But don't worry, that is in your past. Focus on the courage you will show in the future."

"But how can I stop being fearful?" I asked in frustration.

"I am sure you know the answer to that," he replied. "How good did you feel earlier when you visualised your dream of becoming a teacher?"

"Really great."

"Exactly. If you want something bad enough, your imagination will come to your aid. But it must be something that you really want. Your imagination will not help you unless you really want to achieve that dream with all your heart. When that happens, you have something very powerful on your side."

"What's that?"

"Your *passion*, Tom! Passion is what summons courage. Courage is deep inside all of us and passion is what brings it to the surface."

I thought about the word 'passion' and recalled hearing it many times on television when commentators spoke about sportspeople. They often used the word to describe the winner or the winning team. Suddenly it made sense to me. I realised that to win in sport, and in life, you must live with passion. I imagined passion to be like a brave knight that would come to slay fear.

I became very impressed with the turtle's courage, and was open to the possibility that there could be other lessons to be learned from it.

The Turtle's Third Lesson – *Live in your element*

"There is a third lesson we can learn from the turtle," the old man continued. "People think of the turtle as being very slow, but did you know that turtles are actually very fast when they are in their element?"

"Really? What is their element?"

"Water! Turtles can swim under water as fast as we humans can run on land. Their element is the sea, not land. They have to struggle over land to get to the sea. But once they reach it, their progress accelerates. They can go from coast to coast and cover hundreds of kilometres very quickly.

"That is an important lesson for us, Tom. We too must experience some hard work to reach our element. We have to work through some tough goals to achieve our dreams."

"So, what is *our* element?" I asked.

"Humans are unique in that our element is different for each of us. It is only discovered when we take action in the direction of our dreams. When we follow our dreams and unleash our passion, we start to live in our element. We will notice this because time seems to stand still as we become absorbed in what we are doing. We start achieving our goals quickly. And that's when we accelerate our progress in all areas of life."

"I know what my element is," I interrupted. "Teaching!"

"Good for you, Tom. Most people go through life never discovering their element. Now that you have found yours, you can start to pursue it with courage. Your next challenge will be to stay courageous in the face of fears and obstacles that may confront you along the way to being a great teacher. You must learn to keep courage on the surface of your heart and mind. Do you think you know how to do that?"

"By having passion?" I asked.

"Passion is only half the equation," he replied. "Passion does indeed bring courage to the surface of our consciousness but there is something else that keeps it there. Something that holds it in place even after the initial excitement subsides and the reality of hard work dawns on us."

I searched for the answer by trying to think of what else we could learn from the turtle. Nothing came to mind. I even looked up at the eight Trees for inspiration – but still nothing. I knew that visualising my dreams would make me courageous at a time when I needed, but what could possibly make me courageous *all* the time? Especially when I was trying to achieve some very tough goals and performing tasks that are difficult.

Sensing my struggle, the old man said, "That's okay, Tom, this next lesson from the turtle will reveal the answer."

And so it did.

The Turtle's Fourth Lesson – *Willpower*

"The fourth lesson that the turtle teaches us is *willpower*," he said. "What do you think willpower is?"

"Is it like having determination?"

"Yes, you are on the right track. It is one side of the same coin as determination but is infinitely more powerful. Willpower comes from the heart whereas determination comes from the mind. Determination may be followed by frustration but willpower is always followed by strength and peace."

He paused to make a fist and added, "Willpower is what builds discipline to perform tough tasks!

157

"Realising our dreams isn't always fun and exciting, Tom. We have to achieve some very tough goals to get there. When the turtle is on land it can only move slowly, but it never gives up. Like the turtle, we too must take small, sometimes arduous, steps toward our goals and dreams. It takes willpower to not give up.

"Willpower is what helps the turtle make it to the sea. It takes slow steps to get to its element, but when it does get there it speeds through the water. Likewise, when you build your willpower through small daily steps, you will reach a point where you end up flying through your goals and realising your dreams much faster.

"Willpower also builds consistency of action. We cannot achieve our goals unless we do what needs to be done consistently. Visualising our dreams daily does ignite our passion and that is, of course, very important; more important than that, however, is taking consistent action. Willpower is what motivates us to take the daily steps that may not be as exciting as our dreams."

I added, "Yes, my teacher tells me that I must be consistent with my effort at school."

"Exactly, Tom. Otherwise, what is the use if you diligently work towards your goals one day but get distracted by fruitless pursuits the next? That's what most people do. But willpower fixes that."

"How do I build my willpower?" I asked.

"Do the tasks that are difficult to do," he replied. "To be great at anything, you have to do the tough tasks that others shy from.

"Let me tell you about a friend named Hunter who taught me the perfect lesson on building willpower in all areas of life. Hunter is a body builder who owns a gym in the city. I visit him often. One day I asked him, 'How do you make certain exercises look so easy?' He replied, 'I train hard on the very tough exercises. I push myself to complete them. It makes the other exercises seem much easier.'

"I now go to Hunter's gym to be inspired and to do my strength exercises. But most importantly, I go there to build my willpower."

"*You* go to the gym?" I asked.

"Yes, Tom, don't be so surprised," he laughed. "Since my heart attack, my doctor told me that I have to keep my muscles active because it helps to keep my heart strong. I often exercise outside in the open air, but I also visit the gym because I like to talk with Hunter. He inspires me and keeps me motivated."

"So I guess that makes him *your* teacher." I quipped cheekily.

"Indeed it does," he smiled back at me, "but Hunter is more than that. He gives me advice on many areas of life and not just my health. You see, Tom, when you meet a successful person who is focused like Hunter, it usually means that they have been climbing successfully in all areas of life. Whenever you meet such a person, you should be curious about the way they think and act. Often you will find some real wisdom they have learned and are happy to share with you. Hunter is that type of person. As well as a body builder, he is a loving family man with solid values. He treats all people with respect. He extended that respect to an old man like me who walked into his gym with many physical ailments. He did not dismiss me. He spent time to help train my body and build my willpower."

Daily rituals help build willpower

"How did he help you build willpower when you were so frail and had not done any tough exercises before?"

"He did this by teaching me the power of developing a ritual."

"What's a ritual? Is it like habit?"

"A habit is something that you develop without really thinking, whereas a ritual is something that you do with forethought and deliberate purpose. It is something you do regularly so it becomes part of your daily routine.

"Body builders develop their rituals by training their body to perform certain exercises at the same time every day. Some, for example, train first thing in the morning, others late in the afternoon. So guess what would happen if that time of day came around and they missed training? They would feel lost, like something was missing from their day. They have built a ritual for training at that time. Even if that something is tough and challenging, their mind still prompts them to show up. And, showing up to perform a task is half the equation to building willpower. The other half is, of course, performing that task, even if it may be difficult or mundane.

"You can train yourself to do just about anything by turning it into a ritual. You can develop a ritual for learning, by studying at the same time daily. You can also do this for working or for sleeping or eating the right foods or for spending time with your family and friends. Once you have formed these rituals, they become entrenched in your daily life and they become very difficult to break. That's when you will see your willpower in action."

The old man paused and then advised, "There is however one other essential ingredient to the successful practice of courage and willpower – Love!"

Be Motivated by Love

"Love life and life will love you back.
Love people and they will love you back."
Arthur Rubinstein

*A*s we sat underneath those eight magical Trees, I felt a deep connection with the old man. He was kind enough to take the time to teach me all that he had learned. He was honest with his feelings. He cried in front of me and laughed in front of me. He was human. He was caring. Most of all, he was loving.

He taught me that all humans want to love and be loved. Above all, he taught me that love allows courage to manifest itself purely, without aggression.

I was eager to build my willpower and show courage on the soccer field. I could visualise myself practicing daily and improving my skills. I knew that if I acted on my dreams with courage, I would soon be a great player. This newfound focus got me excited.

The old man sensed my restlessness and said, "Follow me, Tom. I want to take you back to the Tree of Love and teach you something very important. You must know this before you start taking action."

We arrived at the Tree of Love and stood there gazing up. There was a long silence. The old man looked like he was reflecting. I was hesitant to speak but finally found the courage to ask, "Is this where you will tell me about the third step in the Circle of Conscious Living? I am excited about everything I have learned and want to learn more. I want to be the best!"

Without looking at me or taking his eyes off one of the branches, he replied, "I love your enthusiasm, Tom, but I am not ready to teach you the next step in the Circle just yet. You have to first learn a very important rule about courage and willpower. It is a rule that, if broken, will undermine the goals and dreams you hope to achieve. The rule is simply this: All your actions must be motivated by *love*. If you want to be the best, then be the best that *you* can be. Don't be the best with the aim of being better than others. Don't be the best so you can fill yourself with pride. Your motivation for achieving your goals and dreams must be love and not to prove a point to others.

"Love is the secret ingredient, Tom, otherwise success will be material and not internal. Internal success is when you achieve something that makes you happy and adds value to other people's live. Doing things out of jealousy, hatred or revenge will not make you happy. It will not give you peace of mind."

"I understand," I responded, "but our soccer coach tells us that 'success is the best revenge'. We lost last year's semi-final to a team who played aggressively to beat us. So this year he told us to get equally as aggressive to avenge that loss."

The old man pondered for a moment and said, "It is fine to play your best game and feel the energy and passion of wanting to win, but you can still be motivated by love."

"Really?"

"Yes Tom, don't be too surprised to learn that the best sporting champions in the world respect and admire their competitors. They put themselves in their shoes and appreciate the courage and willpower that they must possess to compete at the highest level.

"You see, your only real competitor in sport and in life is yourself and your fears. So, it is not about beating others. It is about playing your best game. And if on the day your game is better than your opponent's game, then so it goes that you win."

"But how can you *love* your competitor when you want to beat them?" I asked.

He paused, looked up at the tree above us and answered, "Look up at the Tree of Love, Tom. Notice that there are three branches. There is the Braided Branch of love for your future sweetheart and the branch of unconditional love for your family. Do you see that third branch?"

"Yes."

"Well this branch is the love you should have for all others on this Earth."

"Even strangers?"

"Yes, Tom, even strangers. In life you must love not only the people you know, but more importantly, the people you do not know."

"But my mother tells me to be wary of strangers."

"Yes, but please do not confuse caution with fear. Fear will keep you from showing love and accepting new people into your life, people who may bring laughter and enrich it. Remember what I told you earlier. When you visualise your dreams and focus on your goals, you form a partnership between your heart and your mind; and that helps you make all the right decisions in life. Trust that partnership. Trust that your heart will feel uncomfortable and your mind will tell you when you need to avoid a person.

"But do you know what I've realised in my old age. I've realised that fearing others brings us more trouble than showing love. Since waking up in that hospital bed I have lived with love in my heart. Instead of meeting people with fear and suspicion, I greet them with love and an open heart. This has brought many friends into my life. I have learned that people are wonderful if we just approach them with the warmth and love that they deserve. I have also learned that we get more out of life when we love than when we fear or hate. We have so much more to gain than we could ever lose.

"Fear of unfamiliar people is one of the biggest problems in our world today, Tom. People fear others from different countries. They fear the younger generation. They fear different religions. They fear people who speak a different language. But do you remember what I taught you about fear?"

"Yes, you said it was the enemy of friendship."

"Very good, but do you know what else it is? It is also the enemy of love! It stops us from having the courage to show love towards others. And if we do not have love in our hearts for other people, we stop connecting with them.

"Even friends were once strangers, Tom. So if we never show love towards strangers, we will be turning down so many opportunities to make new friends."

He paused to smile at me, as he so often did, to make sure that I was following his lesson. I was starting to appreciate that the old man really cared for me. I wondered why that was so, when he only just met me. Somehow I knew that the lesson on love had something to do with it.

He then said, "Let me tell you a story about a stranger who, when I first saw him, looked mean and scary. It is a story about the unlikeliest of friendships.

"After my retirement from work, I became disillusioned by my lack of purpose. I tried to add meaning to it by regularly visiting my daughter Penny. On one cold, rainy winter evening, I was travelling home on the train after one such visit.

"I stepped off the train, and as I commenced the long walk down the platform towards the stairs I looked up to notice an unkempt man approaching me from the opposite direction. He looked up at me with a menacing face. 'Is this guy going to mug me?' I thought to myself. As he walked towards me, I returned his stern look. I feared him so I reacted by putting on a face that was equally menacing in an attempt to intimidate him. As I mentioned earlier, Tom, I am not proud of who I was back then. I could be defensive and rude. When I was in public, love was farthest from my thinking. I always thought that love was only reserved for family."

"So what happened?" I asked, with anxious curiosity.

"Well, my heart started beating hard in my chest as we approached each other. Fearing the worst, I stepped a little to my left to avoid his path."

"And then? Did he try to mug you?"

"Actually, nothing happened. He kept walking and I kept walking. I breathed a sigh of relief as I descended the stairs. I was glad to avoid such a scary-looking character.

"But then something happened on those stairs that altered the course of my life forever.

"It was then that I suffered my heart attack, Tom. I collapsed on the stairs and struck my head as I rolled down. The next thing I knew, I woke up in hospital with Sarah and Penny standing beside me."

He paused.

"Do you know who *else* was standing beside me?"

"Who?"

"The same scary man I passed on the platform."

"Really?!"

"Yes, Tom, his name is Andrew. It was he who saved my life. He worked as a nurse in a nearby hospital. He had just finished his shift and was on his way home. He resuscitated me and kept me alive until the ambulance came. I was very lucky that he happened to be passing by. When I collapsed, some people called out to the stationmaster for help. Andrew heard the commotion just as he was about to board the train. He turned around and came to my aid. He could have minded his own business. But he didn't. He had love in his heart."

"Wow that is incredible! Only a few minutes earlier, he gave you a mean look. Why would he then come to your aid?"

"He wasn't mean, Tom. I unfairly formed the wrong judgement of him. He did look scary but how he looked was not reflective of what was in his heart.

"I was in a depressed state that night. Trying to reconnect with Penny was proving to be frustrating, so I was overly sensitive. It was also cold and raining – not the most conducive of conditions to being friendly. Likewise, Andrew had just finished a long shift at work and had witnessed the death of a person in his ward. He had become acquainted with this patient over many days and was understandably heartbroken. He was cold and hungry as he walked onto that train station, and could not help but have a grimace on his face.

"Andrew is now one of my dearest of friends. We visit each other often. We sometimes reflect on that night and how we both thought the other looked scary and unfriendly. We laugh about it but as you can see, Tom, the story serves as an example of how wrong we can be when our first reaction is fear instead of love.

"When our actions are motivated by genuine love, people are drawn to us. That is why I walk around with a ready smile, because I want people to know that the expression on my face is congruent with what is in my heart."

"It is difficult to be friendly to some people," I said, "especially when someone at school teases or bullies me. How can I show them love?"

"The best way to treat people is to remember that everyone has goodness inside of them. Sometimes things happen in a person's life that fills them with negative emotions. Maybe they lost their job. Maybe they had an argument with a friend. Or maybe they are simply having a bad day."

"Or maybe they received a poor result in a school exam," I added.

"That's right, Tom. There is a myriad of things that can befall us throughout our lives. And I have learned that behind every face I come across in the street, there is a story. There is a reason why some people look unfriendly or even miserable."

"And scary!" I chimed in.

"Yes, and scary, Tom," he laughed. "But, you shouldn't let unfriendly people change the way you behave in this world. You should show love whether someone gives it back or not. Otherwise, you will be letting others change the person you are. If someone is being rude or just plain unfriendly, you should not respond in-kind. In fact, we have a greater obligation to show love to such people. It's easy to be nice to someone who is nice to us. True courage comes when we show love and kindness to people who appear to be unapproachable. They are the one's who need our love the most."

"Two wrongs don't make a right, mum always says."

"That's precisely my point. Otherwise, fear and hatred would spread in the world. Fear and hatred would take over from courage and love. And that is not a world worth living in. That's why we must individually break that cycle in ourselves, which will rub off on the people we come into contact with. With love, we can change the world one person at a time."

"How does one show love? It sounds a bit embarrassing."

"It's really not that awkward, Tom. A simple smile and kind words is all it takes."

"But what about when people are *really* mean? People who do the wrong thing by us? How do we show them love?" I asked.

The old man nodded and said, "Of course it would be naïve of me to think that each person we come across has the potential to be our friend. While there are few bad people in the world, they do exist. And of course we must be cautious of these people. But resisting them with feelings of hatred or revenge is not the answer; it will not bring us any joy. It will not change the outcome or undo the wrong that may have been done to us. We must remove such feelings from our heart; otherwise we will hurt ourselves even more. We will become cynical and unhappy. Ultimately it will rob us of our passion. Courage and willpower will then abandon us. And it will be replaced with weakness.

"There will certainly be times where even our best of intentions to show love will not result in love in return. Do you know what we do then, Tom? We *accept* that there are some things in life that we cannot control. Other people's actions is one of them.

"This now leads me to the third step in the Circle of Conscious Living; the step that teaches acceptance. Are you ready to hear it?"

"I certainly am," I replied. I was excited to learn this next step, not only because I would hear more of the old man's stories, but because I anticipated that each step was leading me closer and closer to finding the Garden of Happiness and my way home.

CHAPTER 14

STEP THREE:
Accept what Flows in Life

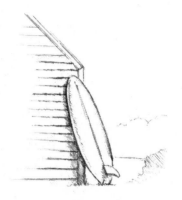

"Happiness can exist only in acceptance."
George Orwell

As the afternoon sun drifted lower in the sky, I thought about the previous lesson and the first two steps in the Circle. I understood the role that goals and dreams played in stimulating passion. And I understood that passion brought courage to the surface so I could push past fear and take action in the direction of my goals. But I stopped to think – what if something bad happened in my life that I could not change? And what if my actions were futile on matters outside my control?

I asked the old man these vexing questions.

"Life sometimes brings us challenges," he said. "At times we can deal with such challenges by taking action with courage; but at other times there is nothing we can do. This is where the third step in the Circle of Conscious Living becomes important to our happiness.

"For most people who do not live by a pattern of positive thinking, this is a difficult step to master. But when you follow the first two steps in the Circle, acceptance becomes much easier. Let me explain how.

"To be able to accept bad things that happen in life, your heart must truly believe that you are doing your best to *live* your life. Otherwise, you will have a burning doubt whether you could have averted these happenings. You may try and convince yourself to accept them, but you will find it difficult because it is impossible to fool the heart, Tom. If the mind knows that you have not been focusing on your goals and that you have not taken action with courage and with love, it is difficult to convince the heart to feel otherwise. The heart knows when you are not doing your best."

"So how do I do my best?" I asked.

"By focusing on your goals and dreams and taking daily action in each of these eight Trees. By following these first two steps in the Circle, you have no choice but to accept what flows, because your heart will believe that there was nothing more that you could have done.

"When I had my heart attack, I suffered the misery of regret. 'Why me?' I kept asking myself as I lay in that hospital bed. Then I started to blame my job and the stress it caused. I even blamed Sarah for not persuading me to eat well and exercise more. I did not accept responsibility for my own actions. I did not accept responsibility for the many years of neglecting my health. That's why I became unhappy – not because I had the heart attack but because I did not take responsibility for what happened to me. And do you know why I could not accept what happened to me? Because I knew deep down that I had not been taking action in the direction of my goals and dreams. I knew that I did not have courage and love in my heart. I knew that I had not been living my best life. If I had been doing all that I could in all areas of my life and still had the heart attack, I could have accepted that."

He paused.

"Can I ask you a question, Tom? When was the last time something bad happened to you that you had no control over? And how did you feel about it?"

"Well, last year my soccer coach did not pick me for the first grade team. Instead he put me in the reserves. I felt like he favoured some of the other players. I sulked to my parents about it. I lost interest and stopped training."

"So, you did not accept his decision?"

"No I didn't. I was so upset."

He gave me a curious "Hmm".

"You see, Tom, you did not accept what happened because deep down you must have felt that you did not do your best. If you did your best and still did not get picked for the first grade team, then I suggest you could have lived with that decision because you would have felt a sense of satisfaction that there was nothing more you could have done. You cannot control your coach's decision, can you? The only thing you can control is your own preparation and training."

The old man was right. The truth was that I really did not train as hard as the other players. I knew deep down that I could do better if I put in more effort. All I could do was accept my coach's decision and try harder next time.

"Why is it important to accept bad things that sometimes happen? Can't I just feel angry during those times?" I asked.

"Yes you can Tom, but what will that achieve? When you do not accept what happens, it paralyses you into inaction. You start to think in a negative pattern. Dwelling on the problem will not highlight the solution. The solution only comes to your mind when your heart has accepted the problem.

"The truth is that when you show anger towards someone else, you are really blaming them for your situation. When you blame others, it means that you are trying to *control* them. Likewise, when you blame a situation, you are trying to control everything that happens in life. You are resisting life itself.

"We cannot fight the force of the world, Tom. We are but a speck on the Earth's surface; who are we to resist these invisible forces that shape our existence? So don't try to control the world, because you will lose. You have to make the world your friend. To do that, you must have the courage to change what you can and accept what you can't. The key to understanding this challenge is to realise that the need to control others or situations comes from fear. And when you fear, you start to run from your problem.

"Let me ask you a simple question. If you came across a grizzly bear in the woods, what would you do?"

"I would run for my life," I laughed.

"That's right. Fear makes you run. And that is natural when we are faced with real danger. But when you feel fear by trying to control everything and by resisting life's happenings, you are also running away. This time, though, you are running, not from a bear, but from the problem itself. And that is not right, is it?"

"No I guess not," I responded.

I reflected on the problem with my soccer coach and realised that there was no use trying to control his decision. I should just focus on doing my best by training harder with courage and willpower.

"Something truly empowering happens when you accept your problems," he continued. "Your heart will feel calm and your mind starts to focus on the solution. You may not be able to change the past but you sure can do your best to shape the future.

"I only learned the wisdom I am sharing with you today because I finally accepted that my heart attack was the result of my own neglect. When that happened, my mind started focusing on the solution. I went back to the second step in the Circle of Conscious Living and put together an action plan to eat better, exercise and relax. I started looking forward with hope, rather than backward with regret.

"There is a time when you have to accept what life brings and not resist it or deny it. There is a time for action and a time for reflection and acceptance. It is no use getting upset about the things that are outside of your control. At these times, you should open up your journal and pour your heart's feelings onto the pages. After you do this you must ask yourself two very important questions.

"First, 'Is there anything I can *do* to fix the problem or meet the challenge?' If so, then you must take action with courage.

"Second, 'If I cannot do anything to fix the problem, is there anything I can *learn* from it?' If so, then at the very least you can prevent it from happening again.

"In both cases, you are *accepting* the challenge and not running away. The only difference is that one requires you to take *action* with courage and the other requires you to *learn* from it and move on.

"The wisdom of knowing when to take action and when to accept comes from journaling. That is why the journal I gave you is so important. When you journal and ask yourself these two questions, your heart and mind will guide you to the answer."

I looked down at the journal that was still in my left hand and felt very fortunate to have it. The old man watched and waited for me as I fanned through the pages. It was like he was anticipating a question that would soon come to me. And so it did.

"What if I have a problem that I can neither fix nor learn

from? What if it made no difference at all?"

"That's a very good question, Tom. I can see that you are thinking very deeply about this issue. Acceptance is indeed a difficult step to master. There is, however, a sport that can guide you to the answer. That sport is surfing."

"Surfing?"

"Yes, Tom. Surfing is truly an amazing sport. It can teach us a lot about acceptance and going with the flow. Surfers know not to resist the force of nature and the chaotic energy of the ocean's waves. Any good surfer will tell you that if you try and resist the wave's force and direction, it will toss you out of the way. So the choice is to either ride it or let it pass.

"Likewise we must journey through life. We must have the courage to get up on our board and ride the waves that we think will bring us happiness. Because waves are like change, the bigger they are, the greater the opportunity for adventure. Sure, some waves may throw us off the board, dumping us in the water. But we must learn to get back up to ride the next one. We must not stay down for too long, otherwise we will miss the next wave of opportunity."

"But what happens if a wave dumps us into the sand and hurts us?" I asked.

"When misfortune occurs outside our control, we must reflect on the lessons without blaming anyone, including ourselves. We have to let it go and trust that something good may come from it in the future. Knowing that you dreamt your best life and acted on your goals with courage is enough. Knowing that you have tried your hardest is all you can do. The rest is left up to *chance*."

"Chance?"

"Yes, Tom, chance can sometimes bring problems but I still prefer to live by it, because there are two positives that also flow from chance. The first is that, just as bad things can happen, so too can good things. The second is that not knowing what happens next in life makes it interesting, even if painful sometimes.

"It would get very boring if everyday was predictable. We would never get to feel excitement. That is why we love to watch sport. We do not know what to expect next in the game. We sit on the edge of our seat in anticipation, and that is what makes it exciting. Life is no different. All we can do is play our best game and leave the rest to chance."

I started imagining a future with endless possibilities and exciting pursuits. But, I also imagined some terrible things that could happen to prevent me from taking action. I watched the news with my father most nights and saw the tragedies that ruin some people's lives. There were many stories of car accidents and occasional stories of airplane crashes. There were also random acts of violence against innocent people. In those stories, there was nothing that the victims could do to avoid the tragedy or learn from it. I found myself unable to comprehend how I would feel if such things happened to me or my family. I would find it very difficult to accept. I would be devastated.

I shared my concern with the old man.

"Tom, I know that life may sometimes bring you heartache, caused by circumstances that you simply cannot change or learn from. If you focus on your goals and dreams, if you take action with courage and love, if you accept what happens in life wholeheartedly and without resistance, then there is nothing more that you can do except to be *grateful* for the life that you *do* have."

He paused and concluded, "Being grateful fixes everything. It is the safety net for your hearts feelings.

"It is also the fourth step in the Circle of Conscious Living."

175

CHAPTER 15

STEP FOUR:
Be Grateful and Giving

When you are grateful, it is easy to give.
When you give, it is easy to be grateful.

Not a day goes by that I do not run through the Circle of
Conscious Living for each area of my life. It is my daily
ritual at sunrise. I visualise my dreams and focus on my goals
in each of my eight Trees. It stirs my emotions and sparks my
thinking. I open my journal and run through the actions I need
to take and remind myself to do so with courage and with love.
I also remind myself that when I give my best, there is nothing
I can do but accept whatever life brings. It is at this point in my
thinking, that a little smile appears on my face.

What the old man taught me, and experience has proven true,
is that happiness is effortless when I follow the steps in the Circle
of Conscious Living. Even if I have setbacks or disappointments,
they do not invade my feelings for very long. The fourth step in

the Circle does not allow that to happen. Gratefulness takes over and happiness is not far behind.

I do not remember and cannot describe in great detail what the old man looked like, but I do recall three things about him that are as vivid as yesterday's memory. They were, his intelligent eyes, his calming voice and the fresh smell of his garment. It smelled just like the sun! So whenever I feel the sun's rays on my face, I recall that scent and everything that the old man taught me about being grateful and being giving.

The Sun

The old man asked me to stand up and walk with him. He took me out of the shade of the eight Trees and into the grassy meadow where the wildflowers were now dancing in the breeze. He asked me to shield my eyes and look up in the direction of the sun.

"I want you to close your eyes, Tom, and take your hands away from your face. Now tell me what do you feel?"

"I feel the sunshine on my face. It is giving me goose bumps," I said with eyes closed and a big smile. The warmth of it felt like being hugged by my mother.

"It feels good, doesn't it?"

"Yes it does."

I opened my eyes and turned to see the old man smiling at me. He said, "Anytime you need cheering up in life you should go outside and feel the warmth of the sun and smile."

I giggled and replied, "What if I am at school? I cannot just go outside whenever I feel like it."

"Why not, Tom? It only takes a couple of minutes and I am sure your teacher would understand; she may even join you. I certainly look up at the sun whenever I need to feel grateful. Sure, some people may stare at me, but the happy feeling I get is far more important to me than the brief sense of embarrassment."

I started to giggle again as I imagined people staring at the old man looking up at the sun.

He chuckled with me and added, "Sometimes when I finish my dose of sunshine, I look back down to notice people standing next to me also gazing upwards, wondering what it is that I am looking at!"

The old man broke out in a fit of laughter. I joined him and laughed so hard that my stomach started to cramp. After what seemed like minutes of laughter, we finally composed ourselves and wiped the tears from our cheeks.

"Oh it's so good to laugh," he said.

"In all seriousness, Tom, the feeling of the sun on your face is the closest feeling to gratefulness you will ever experience."

"Really? What does the sun have to do with being grateful?"

"Well, it is important that you remind yourself to be grateful every day and what better way to do that than to feel the warmth of the sun.

"The miracle of the sun shining is the most amazing thing we should feel grateful for on this Earth, because it supports all life as we know it, including our own. Being alive is the most important thing we can be grateful for. And the sun shining is our daily reminder of that.

"There were many times during my years at work when I needed to feel happy but did not know how to change my thinking. I stayed in my office fretting over problems that made me miserable. It never occurred to me that experiencing happiness was as simple as feeling a sense of gratitude. Now it's as easy as letting the sun bathe my face with warmth. And *that*, Tom, is what reminds me to be grateful."

The old man turned to start walking back to the shade of the eight Trees. I followed diligently. At that instant, a coastal breeze started to blow and it was then that I smelled the freshness of his garment. It smelled just like my mother's linen flowing on a clothesline on a bright sunny day.

As we walked he asked me, "Do you understand the meaning of the word gratefulness?"

"I think I do," I replied. "My father often reminds me of how lucky we are to have a roof over our head and food on the table. When we do not feel like eating our vegetables, he tells my sister and I that there are a lot of children in poorer countries who do not have any food at all."

"That is a wise reminder by your father, Tom. Having food to eat is indeed something we must not ever take for granted. But there is so much more than food we can be grateful for. I am certainly grateful for so many things in my life."

"But you have made so many mistakes and have so many regrets," I said.

As the words came out of my mouth, I realised that I did not think before saying them. I probably hurt his feelings. I blushed and looked down, ashamed.

"It's okay, Tom. I am not hurt by what you said. Being grateful for who I am *now* helps me to stay happy no matter my circumstances and past regrets. I know that I cannot change what I did in the past, but I have total control over what I think and do in the present. Some people may pity me for the heart attack I suffered and the relationships I took for granted; but that is in my past and I do not live in the past. I live my life daily and I have a lot to be grateful for, right now, at this very moment."

"Really?"

"Yes, Tom. Every day is my best day. No one can ever make me feel otherwise. I wake up every morning and look at the sun to remind myself that I am alive. I don't focus on regrets.

Their circumstances are gone. I have learned to accept that part of my life. It led me to where I am now. I am even grateful that I had the heart attack."

"How could you be grateful for that?"

"Because had I not endured such a painful period, I would never have discovered the lessons I am sharing with you today. I would not have made any changes in my life. Therefore, the heart attack was the best thing to happen to me at that point in time. And living to see the dawn is the best thing that happens to me daily. That is why the sun gives me reason to smile. It reminds me that I am still alive and able to enjoy the wonder of living on this beautiful Earth of ours.

"We must never take the simple things for granted, Tom. The first thing I took for granted was my own life. I thought I had all the time in the world to achieve my goals and dreams. But the heart attack reminded me that life is fleeting. So now, I remind myself daily that today could be my last day. I could die tomorrow."

"Doesn't that make you feel sad?"

"On the contrary, it motivates me to keep climbing and reminds me to pursue my goals *now* instead of later. And when I fill my day with positive pursuits, I do not have time to feel sad."

He paused to reflect and added, "Happiness is not some random mystery that comes and goes, Tom. It can be achieved by following a positive pattern of thinking, like the one I am teaching you today. Happiness can be *learned*."

"How?" I asked.

"By following this fourth step in the Circle and listing all the things you should be grateful for in your life."

"I know I must have a lot of things to be grateful for, but how do I think of them? Where should I start?"

"Everything you ever need to be grateful for is in these eight

Trees, Tom. If you look in the Tree of Health you can be grateful that you have eyes to see, ears to hear and a nose to smell. You can be grateful for your taste buds and the amazing array of food that is out there for you to taste. You can be grateful for the energy you have to go to school and to play sport. You can be grateful for the time you have to relax and rejuvenate each evening.

"In the Tree of Love and the Tree of Family, you can be grateful that you have parents who love you and care for you. You can be grateful that you have a sister to talk to and share good times with.

"In the Tree of Learning, you can be grateful for the opportunity to get an education. You can be grateful that you live in a generation with access to so much technology that makes learning interesting and effortless. And you can be grateful for the many books that are available for you to read.

"In the Tree of Work, you can be grateful for the privilege of working and serving others. You can be grateful that you were born with certain talents and skills. You can be grateful that you get to display these talents at work.

"In the Tree of Wealth, you can be grateful that you live in a country where you have the freedom and opportunity to accumulate wealth.

"In the Tree of Charity, you can be grateful for the many charitable organisations that provide you the opportunity to show your generosity.

"Finally, you have much to be grateful for in the Tree of Friendship. One of the most important things to be grateful for is the people in your life. Having friends and family, people you can talk to, laugh with, and cry with, is one of life's greatest comforts.

"You see, Tom, when you really think about it, there are so many things you can be grateful for. The list is endless. They are like nuggets of gold hidden beneath the surface in your heart and mind. You will find them by focusing on what you have and on the simple things that come into your life."

"I can be grateful that I met you today," I said happily.

"Thank you, Tom, that means a lot to me."

The Two Imposters

I started to imagine everything that I could be grateful for. It *did* put a smile on my face. The smile came without me noticing.

"Why does feeling grateful make us so happy?" I asked.

"Because gratefulness precedes happiness," he answered and paused for me to understand.

He gave me a curious look and added, "You must be wary, however, that there are two imposters who disguise themselves as happiness but will lead you astray. They drive a wedge between you and gratefulness, and ultimately take away your happiness. I want you to be on the lookout for them."

"Two imposters?" I imagined two men in disguise with dark clothing. They would steal people's happiness and store it in a big black bag.

"These two imposters are, in fact, creations of our own mind, Tom; our own negative thinking," he clarified.

"The first imposter is the one who orders you to take all the wonderful things in your life for granted. The second is the one who tells you to focus on what you do *not* have. These imposters will trick you into ignoring what you have and make you pursue what you don't have, on the false promise that it will make you happy. I have known many people who have had every reason to be grateful and happy but because they listened to and followed these two imposters, they led an unhappy life.

"I want to tell you a story about one such person, Tom. It is as much an inspirational tale as it is cautionary."

I shifted to get comfortable. I enjoyed the old man's stories.

"Later in my career, I had the opportunity to meet the owner of the company I worked for. His name was Bob. We got to know each other well and I began to be invited to functions where Sarah and I met his family, including his daughter, Jessica.

"Jessica was a well-loved daughter who had everything anyone could hope for. She went to one of the best private schools in the state. She shopped for clothes at expensive boutiques. She ate at the best restaurants with her friends. Her father even bought her a flashy convertible. She was an only child with the undivided attention of both parents. The problem with Jessica, however, was that she was ungrateful for all those things.

"One day after work, Bob confided in me that his daughter was never happy. He was very frustrated because he felt he could not connect with her, no matter how hard he tried.

"You see, Tom, Jessica was never happy because she focused constantly on what she did not have. Every time she bought something new, she would be happy while the excitement lasted, but as she grew bored with it she became unhappy again.

"Jessica took all the simple but important areas of her life for granted. She took her health and energy for granted. She took her parents for granted. Her house. Her school. Her friends. Her car. The food she ate. The clothes she wore. The country she lived in. Just about everything.

"This lack of gratefulness caused her to focus on the negative qualities in people, including herself. It got to the stage where even buying new things would not make her happy. She started turning her negativity on herself. She began to focus on her flaws rather than her talents and strengths. She was a brilliant pianist, a beautiful dancer and a creative fashion designer. She also had a wonderful ability to connect with children. But she did not see any of those qualities, nor did she show them. She started to hate herself."

"Really? How can you hate yourself? That sounds silly."

"It *is* silly, but that is exactly what can happen if you do not have gratefulness in your heart. At first you may think that it only affects others but, as Jessica's story will reveal, it can potentially ruin your life.

"As time went on, Jessica's unhappiness developed into an eating disorder. She became very ill."

"What's an eating disorder? Is it when someone stops eating?"

"Yes it could be. For some, it is about their appearance and a diet that goes too far. For others, their weight may be the one thing in their life that they can control, when everything else seems out of control. In Jessica's case, she stopped eating food as a form of punishment to herself because she felt inadequate. She lost confidence in herself and felt like she had nothing to contribute to the world. The eating disorder was her heart's cry for help."

"So what happened to her?" I asked with heartfelt concern, as I imagined if my own sister Sophia went through such misery.

"I saw Bob recently. In fact, we still visit each other regularly, even though we are both retired. We sit and reflect on old times and the lessons we have learned. He was relieved to tell me that Jessica was healthy and happy again. He was also very excited to share with me the most amazing story on how she got better. It was not an easy journey but one with a very happy ending."

"How did she get better? What did she do to feel happy again? Did Bob teach her to be grateful?" I asked with a barrage of questions.

"Very good, Tom. I can see that you are always thinking of how you can apply the lessons I am teaching you. But I learned that an eating disorder is a very serious illness that cannot be fixed simply by *telling* someone to be grateful. The love and support of her parents certainly aided her recovery but it was

Jessica herself that learned to be grateful for all of her wonderful qualities and the life she had the opportunity to live. In turn, and importantly, she began to love herself and *that* helped her to overcome the illness."

"How did she do that?"

"By changing her *thinking*," the old man pointed to his temple poignantly.

"Let me explain how. It is such an inspiring story of a parent's love and the power of being grateful and giving.

"Bob and his wife never gave up on their daughter. At first, they sent her to the best doctors and clinics that specialised in treating eating disorders. But none of them seemed to make a difference. Being away from home made Jessica sad. While she improved little by little, the fact that she missed her family kept her from fully recovering. She needed love. She needed to be with her parents."

He paused momentarily. I wondered whether he was thinking of Penny. I also felt a sense of sadness overwhelm me as I remembered that I too missed my family. I looked up into the genuine eyes of the old man and my sadness was soon replaced with a sense of hope. I trusted that I would soon find my way home if I continued to focus on what he was saying.

"Being grateful is a powerful force, Tom," he continued. "It can transform your thinking and therefore your feelings. And the more grateful you are the more happiness you receive in return.

"You cannot fool happiness. It will not shine through if you do not truly *feel* gratitude, because gratitude comes from the heart, even though it is guided by the mind."

"How do I know if I am feeling it from the heart?" I asked.

Giving

"There is one simple test for gratefulness, and it is something that I have witnessed time and time again. Truly grateful people are the most *giving*."

"Do you mean they are charitable?"

"Yes, Tom. When you are genuinely grateful for what you have, you are happy to give. In fact, your heart pours out the giving because it just cannot be contained. When you are grateful and happy for your life, you want others to feel the same because being grateful and being giving come from the same place in the heart. You cannot feel one without the other."

He paused.

"But *here* is the important lesson I learned from Bob. The opposite also applies! It is easy to feel grateful *when* you are giving.

"Bob tried many times to help his daughter feel grateful, but she was so sick that she could not comprehend what she could be grateful for. Bob then realised that he could teach his daughter to be grateful by first teaching her to be giving. He believed that if he could show Jessica how much she could give to the world, she would see her true value. She would see the beauty within her.

"What a wonderful piece of wisdom that is, Tom. It was this wisdom that saved his daughter's life. When Bob thought of it, he drove all the way to the clinic where his daughter was being treated. He helped to pack her clothes and they drove straight to the airport. Jessica was a little anxious by the suddenness of her fathers plan but she was also curious about where he was taking her. When they reached the airport, he purchased two tickets to India and they both left that evening."

I interrupted to ask, "Did she learn to be grateful when she arrived in India and saw that there were people much poorer than her?"

"That's what I thought at first, but Jessica's problem was not that she needed to see people worse off than she was. Even though she was ungrateful for all she had, her problem had become much deeper. She no longer felt important or valued. In fact, she felt worthless. The trip to India helped her see how amazing her contribution to life could be if she gave herself the opportunity to help others in need."

"Why, what did she do in India?"

"Jessica and her father volunteered to help at a children's orphanage, Tom. Bob's company had been sponsoring the orphanage for many years. They reached for the Tree of Charity and focused on giving something back to children who needed not only money, but connection.

"Bob ensured that Jessica's days were filled with enriching activities that left no time for her to focus on herself. They ate the same food as the orphans and lived in the same accommodation. Bob worked side by side with his daughter, playing with the children, teaching them to read, and helping the managers of the orphanage. As the days went by, Jessica's confidence began to grow as she saw the huge impact she was having on the children's lives. By helping them, she began to help herself."

"Did she start to eat again?"

"Yes she did, Tom. She began to get stronger. She smiled more. She believed in herself. She learned gratefulness through giving. She became grateful for the wonderful qualities she possessed, for the love of her father and for the opportunity to give of herself and her time to the beautiful children. She also saw how they managed to play, laugh and smile despite their circumstances. And she appreciated the children for who they were, not for what they had. She began to appreciate this quality in herself as well.

"Even Bob learned a lesson from the trip. He told me that

although he was a wealthy man by the measure of money, he felt poor in comparison to the children. They were wealthy in human spirit. Happiness came naturally to them because they were innately grateful.

"For their evening meal, they would gather around to help in setting up the tables. After they ate, they would all help to clean up. And after all was eaten and cleaned, they would sing songs and dance together with smiles as big as their hearts. That was their way of celebrating life and being grateful. They focused on what they had, rather than on what they didn't have. Their outlook had a lasting impact on Bob and Jessica, who since, have been eternally grateful for what the children taught them. To this day, Jessica still visits the orphanage regularly and Bob's company continues to make donations to keep it running."

The old man looked at me with a big smile. He looked as pleased as I was by the happy ending. He added, "When we have trouble feeling grateful, we need to experience *giving* first. It's the long way home to happiness but sometimes it is the only way.

"Happiness isn't about living a perfect life, Tom. There is no such thing. We are all imperfect and we all face challenging circumstances. The key lies in what we focus on. When we focus on what we have and what we should be grateful for, we will be happy despite our circumstances.

"There are certainly days when I find it difficult to be grateful. On such days I think of Jessica's story. It reminds me of all the things I should be grateful for, even when it is cloudy and there is no sun to shine on my face."

CHAPTER 16

STEP FIVE:
Be Fearless and Adventurous

*"Only with absolute fearlessness
can we slay the dragons of mediocrity
that invade our gardens."*

George Lois

Many parents dread the nightly ritual of putting their children to bed, but I do not. It makes me smile because it tells me that my children have an adventurous spirit. That is why they resist going to sleep. I try to tame that spirit for just one night by telling them magical stories to kindle sweet dreams. It is almost sad to see them drift off. But I know that sleep will replenish their energy and the sunrise will bring more excitement into their lives.

As children, we think of so much we can be doing. We see life as one big adventure waiting to unfold. We crave new experiences and fun.

I live my life with that same sense of excitement for what could be; a sense that something is waiting for me on a higher branch if I just reach for it. This feeling prompts me to think of new ideas, try new experiences and meet new people. Adventure makes me feel alive, and the more I feel alive the more grateful I am for my life and the happier I become.

It is difficult to feel grateful for your life if you are not living it. It may sound like a contradiction but it was on that sunny spring afternoon that the old man taught me the difference between life and living; and between being alive and living your best life. He taught me about the two warriors of the human spirit. He taught me about fearlessness and adventure.

The Two Warriors

The afternoon sun was slowly setting and I started to feel anxious about finding my way home before dark. My heart started to crave my mother's open arms and the smell of her cooking. I yearned for the solace of my room and soft bed. I missed my sister Sophia and I missed playing ball games with my father in the front yard.

I anxiously said to the old man, "I have enjoyed our time together and I am thankful for all the lessons I have learned, but I really need to get home. It will be dark soon."

"I know you miss your family, Tom. We do not know how much we miss and love our family until we are away from them. But do not worry. I am certain you will find your way home after you have learned the last step in the Circle of Conscious Living. This is the step that completes our journey together. We will part after this lesson but I leave you with two warriors who will lead you home and guide you throughout your life."

"Warriors?" I turned my head to see if there was anyone else coming to take me home.

"These are not warriors you can see, Tom. They are warriors of the heart, and we all have them deep inside of us."

He paused to face me, stood taller and said with a strong confident voice, "I call these two warriors, *fearlessness and adventure*!"

He put his right hand on my shoulder like a king would on a knight and added, "You are a warrior, Tom. You were born as one. In fact, we are all born fearless and adventurous, but as we grow older our fear grows and our adventure diminishes. The two warriors abandon us and that's when we start to lose our way. You need to be wary of that. You need to keep these two warriors by your side wherever you go in life because they will lift you up to reach for your highest goals and dreams. They will make you feel like anything is possible if you just reach for it. And you will achieve greatness in all areas of your life."

The old man's words filled me with strength and I noticed myself standing taller. I felt something inside of me awaken. I felt like a warrior! I wanted to know how I could keep that feeling with me always.

"How do I keep these two warriors by my side?" I asked.

"You must *practise* being fearless and adventurous," he answered.

"How do I do that?" I was anxious to know because I had a feeling that the answer would guide me back home.

"Please allow me to answer your question with a question. How do you think you will feel when you focus on your goals and dreams daily, take action with courage and love, accept what flows and be grateful and giving in all eight areas of your life?"

"I think I will feel like I can do anything!"

"Excellent, Tom! Your answer tells me that you are following the pattern of thinking in the Circle. Your mind is leading your heart in the right direction. It is making you fearless. And being fearless will unleash your adventurous spirit. You will start to try new things and discover new goals and dreams. That's how the Circle completes itself and leads us back to step one where we started, with new beginnings."

The old man became animated with enthusiasm.

"Let me tell you why adventure is important in our life, Tom. There is a difference between being alive and living. Being alive is an opportunity to live. It is not living. Living an exciting life can only happen when we have a sense of adventure in our heart. Adventure is what takes us outside our comfort zone and exposes us to new opportunities for growth.

"Most people think of adventure as participating in thrilling sports, but really, adventure can be experienced whenever and wherever our senses are stimulated. When we try something new, we are showing fearlessness. Whether it's a new food, new travel, a new sport, a new friend, a new job, and a new love. That is how we discover ourselves and what we are capable of. Without adventure, we would never get to experience our greatness!

"Adventure leads to living, because when we try something new we are stepping into unknown and unfamiliar territory. When that happens, our body's five senses are stimulated."

He paused then added with thoughtful precision, "Living life is felt and measured by the sum total of our senses."

"Our senses?"

"Yes Tom. Do you know what your five senses are?"

"Yes of course. They are seeing, touching, smelling, hearing, and tasting," I recounted proudly, having just learned it at school.

"Very good. Well, when our five senses experience the same thing every day, they become dull. They become too familiar with the known. People call that their comfort zone when in reality it is their dead zone. It is where their senses go to die. But when we have variety and adventure in our life, our senses come alive. They are stimulated. We too then come alive and experience living with passion and excitement!"

For some reason the old man's comments made me recall how enthusiastic and alive I felt when my family last went on holidays.

"Does travelling stimulate the senses?" I asked.

"Absolutely. When we travel to another country, our senses are stimulated by new experiences. It may be the aromas of exotic herbs and spices, seeing new sites, feasting on new food or hearing new music from another culture."

"Or feeling snow or sand between our fingers," I added.

"Exactly, our senses crave *all* such experiences. But we should never wait for holidays to feel that sense of adventure. Every day is an opportunity for adventure."

"Every day? But my father tells me that I am too adventurous and that it will one day get me into trouble. I guess he is right because I was being adventurous when I came into the woods and look where that led me. I am now lost."

"I understand how you feel. Being adventurous does lead us into unknown territory sometimes, but it also leads us to new discoveries. Just think of the wisdom you have learned today. You wouldn't have learned any of it had you not ventured into the woods to climb this tree."

I was willing to entertain the idea that my being lost was somehow positive. I took hope in the fact that the old man's lesson on adventure was perhaps leading me closer to finding my way home. I listened on intently, sensing that he was about to reveal a clue.

True Fearlessness Is Not Recklessness

"As I said, Tom, being fearless awakens our adventurous spirit. But this spirit must be tempered with caution. Being fearless does not mean having no fear. Everyone experiences fear. It is a part of who we are as humans. It is a signal that danger or discomfort might be ahead if we continue a course of action. It is our cue to proceed with vigilance. That's why you should never ever ignore your fear. It will serve you well if you learn how to manage it."

Knowing that feeling fear was a normal part of life made me feel strong. Hearing that I could control it made me feel even stronger.

"How do I manage it?" I asked.

"By using your heart and mind, Tom. You must use that partnership to distinguish between genuine fearlessness and pure recklessness. To do that you must follow the first four steps in the Circle of Conscious Living. Only when you live by every step in the Circle, will the true essence of fearlessness manifest itself in you. You must not break even one of those steps."

The old man paused to reflect. "Your age is a wonderful one for adventure, Tom, but it is also a time of untold danger if you are reckless. I want to tell you a story that demonstrates what can happen if you fail to follow every step in the Circle.

"When I was a boy, I had a friend named Jim. Jim and I spent most of our spare time together. One day when we were walking home from school, we were approached by three older students who started bullying us. They threatened to beat us up unless we handed over our bags. Jim was a feisty young boy who never backed down from a fight, so he refused to hand it over. He got into a scuffle with one of the boys who punched him in the nose. Jim fell to the ground while they ran away with our bags. He picked himself up and became very angry. He found a big stick on the ground and started running after them as they scurried off in a fit of laughter. I followed, pleading with him to forget about it, but he would not listen. He was enraged and wanted revenge.

"While he ran after them, I ran after him. They ran into a thick part of the woods and managed to cross a torrential river by walking across a log. When they got to the other side they dislodged and rolled the log into the river so we could not cross.

"I finally caught up to Jim and we both stood there while they taunted us from the other side. Jim was furious. He took off his shoes and started taking off his clothes. He was going to swim across the river! I pleaded with him not to. I pulled on his arms but he brushed me aside and jumped in to cross to the other side. The other boys' laughter stopped as we all watched Jim struggling to stay above the fierceness of the torrent. It all happened so quickly that no one had time to help him; we just watched him get swept away."

The old man paused and looked down. "I never saw Jim again," he said in a sad voice. "He died in that river. He was my best friend. We did everything together but then he was gone in an instant."

We both fell silent. The story did not need an explanation. I realised how important it was to follow all the steps in the Circle. I had learned enough from the old man to know that Jim's actions were not motivated by love. He showed courage but he was motivated, instead, by revenge.

"But how could Jim have been motivated by love for someone who had just beaten him up and stolen his bag?" I asked in frustration.

The old man turned to me and said, "There is nothing that ever justifies compromising our love for others. Those three boys were brothers that lived in an old shack of a house in the woods. They were fatherless and poor. They had little by way of food. Most winters they had no warm clothing. They stole our bags in the hope they would find some leftover lunch or some clothes to wear. At Jim's funeral, they all stood together and sobbed over his death.

"I tell you this story, Tom, because I care deeply for your future. You are a bright young boy who can make a great contribution to society. I would hate for that to be wasted by one act of impulsive and misguided fearlessness."

Fear as a Barometer

He paused to think and then asked, "Do you know what a barometer is?"

"Yes" I responded, knowing this from my love of meteorology.

"Well, fear is our internal emotional barometer that measures the level of danger or discomfort. When the level of fear gets too high, our body gives us a warning signal like a racing heart or sweaty palms or a feeling in the pit of our stomach that something is just not right. We must learn to pay attention to these signals because it reflects what is going on inside our heart and mind. The problem is that as we grow older, our barometer may not work as well and can give us distorted readings of fear. We start to fear things that we shouldn't. Even simple things like saying hello to people, because we fear rejection. So the risk seems much higher than it actually is."

"Why does this happen?" I asked.

"Because as we get older some of us stop focusing on our goals and dreams; we stop taking action with courage; we stop being motivated by love; we resist and do not accept what flows; we are not grateful for our life and the people in it; and we are not giving of our time and ourselves to others. When we do not consciously follow these preceding steps, Tom, we risk slipping into a lazy and negative circle of thinking. That's when our internal barometer of fear becomes distorted and we stop seeking adventure. We cease to find and focus on new goals and dreams. Our Circle stops flowing and we stagnate. We stop climbing higher in each of our eight Trees. In fact, we start to lose sight of them. It is only when we live with fearlessness in each of them that we get to experience adventure.

"In the Tree of Health, we can be fearless by trying a new

exercise regime or a new sport.

"In the Tree of Love, we can be fearless by shedding our fear and introducing ourselves to someone that we really like.

"In the Tree of Family, we can be fearless by putting our family's interests first and saying 'no' to the things that unreasonably take us away from home.

"In the Tree of Work, we can be fearless by going after a job we love rather than one that pays well.

"In the Tree of Friendship, we can be fearless in making new friends and being ourselves around them.

"In the Tree of Learning, we can be fearless by speaking up and sharing our ideas.

"In the Tree of Wealth, we can be fearless by resisting the temptation to buy things just to keep up with people who boast about their latest material possessions.

"In the Tree of Charity, we can be fearless by volunteering in places that might make us uncomfortable."

As he listed the ways we can practise fearlessness, I began to make a list of my own in my mind. Although I felt excited and confident, I was also a little apprehensive about taking action. It was then that the old man shared with me the most empowering lesson on being fearless.

Adventure Makes You Fearless

"If you find that your internal barometer of fear is holding you back, Tom, there is another simple way to keep it working accurately. Just like fearlessness leads you to adventure, so too does adventure lead you back to fearlessness. The two go hand in hand," he said as he brought both his hands together, as if in prayer.

I started to think back on all the previous steps in the Circle and noticed that each piece of wisdom was made up of two parts that supported the other perfectly. To be *giving* I had to be *grateful* and to be *grateful* I had to be *giving*. It takes *courage* to show *love* and it takes *love* to show *courage*. And now I learned that to be *adventurous* I had to be *fearless* and to be *fearless* I had to be *adventurous*. I was fascinated by the intelligence of this perfectly balanced wisdom.

"So being adventurous will automatically make me fearless?" I asked.

"Yes, Tom. Be adventurous and your fearlessness will not be far behind. Push past your fear. Tell it to 'get out of the way' while you seek adventure"

"What type of adventure must I seek?"

"At your age, everyday is an adventure. Meeting new friends is an adventure. Reading a new book is an adventure. As you get older your idea of adventure will change as you expand your world. You might decide to visit a poorer country to help a charitable organisation. Or simply go hiking through awe-inspiring terrain."

"What do you do for adventure?" I asked. I was curious.

"For me, travelling is the best type of adventure. I always return home feeling fearless after I experience new cultures. It sharpens my internal barometer and makes me open to try new things and meet new people. I love meeting people, Tom. It is an adventure that inspires me the most."

The old man stared into the open meadow momentarily as if he was imagining a far away place.

Power of Mantras

He broke from his daydream and added, "I appreciate that, at your age, it may be difficult to go travelling regularly. So I am going to teach you another simple yet powerful way to be fearless, daily.

"I want to teach you about the power of *mantras*."

"What are they?" I asked.

"Mantras are powerful words you say aloud to yourself that resonate in your heart and in your mind, Tom. They make you *feel* fearless."

"Talk to myself? Aloud?" I laughed.

"At first I thought it was silly too," he chuckled, "but it will keep your fear barometer functioning properly. As I said earlier, we talk to ourselves internally all the time, so we may as well do it consciously and say the right things.

"I first learned about the power of mantras when I met Hunter from the gym. Hunter is the body builder I told you about earlier.

"When I visited his gym I walked around and observed, trying to figure out whether I liked the atmosphere. That's when I observed Hunter lifting weights. At the time I did not know that he was the owner but I was drawn to his corner of the gym because of the powerful words I heard being repeated by him over and over. I noticed that just before he lifted a weight, he would say words like, 'Think strong! Think strong! I can do this! I can do this!'. It was then that I witnessed and truly learned the power of mantras."

I started thinking about the athletes and ball players I watched on television. I recalled how some would mouth to themselves just before they were about to kick the ball. I was always curious about what it was they were saying. They must have been repeating their own mantras.

"What mantras do you say to yourself?" I asked, hoping to learn some of my own.

"I have written many, Tom. At first I had mantras that I would use at the gym; ones that Hunter taught me. But now I also apply them to every area of my life. I repeat them to myself when I first wake up and before I go to sleep. I also say them at times when I need to sharpen my fearlessness, especially when I am faced with a particularly difficult challenge."

He looked at me and realised that I was anxiously trying to think of my own mantras. He smiled at me and asked, "You want to be fearless don't you, Tom?

"Yes sir. I don't like being afraid. I want to be brave just like the athletes I see on television."

He looked at me with gentle eyes and said, "You will, Tom. I promise you that when you write daily in the journal I gave you, your mantras will come to you effortlessly and you will start to feel like a warrior.

"In the Tree of Health, your mantra could be: 'My body is strong and full of energy'. In the Tree of Family, your mantra could be 'I love my family unconditionally'."

"Oh, I understand," I replied. "In the Tree of Learning, my mantra could be: 'I am curious and love to learn'."

"Very good, Tom. That is an excellent mantra," he responded, "but it is also in the *way* you say your mantras that is just as important as what you say. It must be felt in the heart. Would you like me to show you how I say my mantras?"

"Yes please."

"Here goes," he said and closed his eyes. His voice became firm as he started speaking.

"I am fearless because my body is strong and my mind is stronger.

"I am fearless because I focus on my goals and dreams.

"I am fearless because I have the courage to take action to move towards my goals.

"I am fearless because I have the wisdom to deal with anything that life throws at me.

"I am fearless because I embrace change!" he finished with a powerful voice.

He opened his eyes and looked at me with a big smile. He appeared to look bigger, stronger and fearless!

Embracing Change

"When we live with fearlessness and venture into the unknown, we also experience change in our life," he continued. "And sometimes change can be unsettling. It can be fearful. It can frighten us back into our shell."

"But we must be like the turtle," I said eagerly. "We must have the courage to come out of our shell and seek adventure."

"Exactly, Tom. I like your enthusiasm. As I said earlier we must think of change like the waves on a beach. Waves of adventure and opportunity come into our life daily. Just like a surfer, we can choose to ride them or else they leave us behind. Most people let them pass because they are afraid of where the change will take them. They prefer the comfort of their known zone. Their dead zone! They choose to sit and wait for the right wave to come along, and end up waiting their whole life. They think that a safe adventure will eventually come their way."

"Do they wait for a small wave that is safe to ride?" I asked.

"Yes, but in reality no one can ever predict whether a wave is safe or not. In fact, the biggest waves of change often bring the most adventure and the most opportunity for living. We must never take them for granted. Otherwise we will be left with a swamp of stagnant water where there are no opportunities for excitement and growth. That's when we notice that the waves of change have left us behind and we are left like a rudderless boat drifting along aimlessly on the surface of broken dreams."

The old man looked at me intently and his eyes seemed to be holding back the force of a thousand waves. I sat there, spellbound with eyes wide open. He noticed that I was mesmerised, smiled and softened his tone.

"I know I am very passionate about this message, Tom," he said, "but I care deeply for your future and would hate to see you living a small life with no excitement or adventure. It would be a tragedy. In fact, it would break my heart. I have known many who wait their whole life for a safe wave. They let so many pass them by. But as they grow older, they realise that there are no more waves coming their way. No more opportunities to work in a new job or enrol in a new course or travel to a new place. No more opportunities to dream and no more opportunities to experience adventure. They wake up one day and realise that they have wasted their whole life."

He paused in reflection and added in a somber voice, "I was once one of those people."

"That sounds very sad," I said.

"It *is* sad. It is even sadder to learn that, to a lot of people, that's their idea of *living*. They do the same thing every day. They live in their shell, in their comfort zone where there is no risk of failure and no chance for success. I call that a 'nothing' life, Tom. One where you are neither happy nor sad but stuck somewhere in the middle, where you wander through life without any passion or purpose."

"If you were once like that, then why are you so different now?" I asked. "Did you eventually ride your wave of change?"

"I was one of the lucky ones. I had a wave that swept me up and carried me away with it; a wave that I could not avoid. My heart attack was my wave of change.

"You see, Tom, there are two types of change: the change that we seek and the change that is thrust upon us. There are some waves that are too big and too forceful to ignore. They sweep into our lives whether we like it or not. We can choose to ride them and let them take us on an adventure or we can be tumbled and dumped by them. The choice is ours. *I* choose to get up on that board and try to ride that wave."

The old man jumped to his feet and made out like he was riding a surfboard. 'Wow,' I thought to myself. This was not the same old and frail man I first met. He had these moments where he came alive and appeared to be a lot younger. I liked that about him. I liked how he surprised me with his energy.

"Riding those waves of change lead us to new adventures and to new dreams," he continued. "After I left the hospital armed with my newfound wisdom, I *chose* to be adventurous. I forged new friendships. I spent a lot of time mending my relationship with Sarah and Penny. I even started teaching. I grew my own vegetables and learned how to cook nutritious meals. I tried new exercise routines like yoga. I did weight lifting at the gym. I took up road cycling. I tried many new things. I did so with fearlessness. I did not care about looking awkward. I did not care about being ridiculed. I went for it! It brought many new people into my life and helped me to discover new goals and dreams.

"In fact, my latest goal is to complete the Tour de France course."

"Really?" I responded in surprise. I had watched that race on television with my father who also liked to cycle. I knew it was one of the toughest and most gruelling sporting events in the world.

"I know what you are thinking," he said; "that I am too old for such an event. Of course, I am not competing in it, I am just happy to finish it in my own time. Like I said, I am not afraid to try new things. I would never have discovered this goal if I did not first try cycling. I see every day as an adventure to *learn* something new, *do* something new and *meet* someone new. I think that I will get to meet lots of new friends on this new cycling adventure and I am looking forward to learning a new language and trying new food."

I couldn't even begin to imagine how the old man would complete that long cycle course, but I was starting to feel a deep sense of respect for his brave outlook. I imagined him cycling up those hills in the French Alps with that fearless determination in his youthful and enthusiastic eyes.

I looked at him in admiration and asked, "What is it that makes you so fearless?"

Without hesitation he replied, "I am not afraid to fail! I believe that to do nothing is to fail. I choose to do something. *And* I am not afraid of change. I embrace it. Knowing that I have the wisdom of the eight Trees to guide me, and the Circle of Conscious Living to strengthen my heart and mind, gives me confidence. It's like having an army of warriors by my side, ready to pick me up if I fall. That's why I am not afraid, because I know I can get back up. If a wave of change dumps me, my two inner warriors help me to get back up on my board, ready to ride the next wave.

"I have known no other formula for life that is more powerful, Tom. That is why I am sharing it with you. I want you to live like a warrior.

"There are some amazing people in this world, and they all have one thing in common: they are all adventurous. They pursue their dreams with fearlessness."

The old man searched for my eyes, smiled and added, "I think that one day you will be like one of these people. You have the potential and now you have the wisdom that I have shared with you. The rest I leave in your hands."

I looked up at him and our eyes met. His kind eyes were sparkling with the look of adventure. With the setting sun behind him, his clothes were shining brightly. The leaves in the eight trees above us began to rustle as the coastal breeze blew stronger to greet dusk. I looked at the trees and then back at him. His face glowed with a smile that said it was time to say goodbye and time for me to go home. I longed to do so but felt sad to have to part.

Without saying a word, the old man started walking away. I followed a few steps behind him and called out, "Wait up! Where do I go? How do I find my way home?"

"You are an adventurous boy, Tom, so *be* adventurous. You also love to climb."

He kept walking away, his voice growing distant. I didn't know whether I was sad to see him go or apprehensive about being left alone.

I called out to him, "Will I ever see you again?"

He did not respond even though I was certain he could hear me.

There were so many thoughts racing through my mind. The stories. The people. The lessons.

I walked a few more steps in his direction and called out to him again. "Wait. What is your name? You didn't tell me your name."

"It is Thomas, but my friends call me Tom," he yelled back from the distance.

His reply took me by surprise. I wondered why he did not tell me that we shared the same name. I stood there for many moments pondering his mysterious appearance on a day where I desperately needed guidance.

I turned to look at the meadow. I felt isolated and yet, somewhat confident. I looked up to notice that I was standing under the Tree of Family. I smiled and walked towards the trunk and started to climb. I climbed with ease. I reached for each branch with purpose. As I climbed, I felt strong with a sense of anticipation and excitement to reach the top. I strangely felt like my home would be within reach if I were fearless enough to keep climbing.

I felt myself getting closer and closer. I reached halfway up the tree and looked out to see the coast in the distance and the hillside to my right. I could see that the sun was about to set behind the hills. The hills looked a little familiar to me and I could almost make out the tops of some houses. Could one of them be mine?

I kept climbing some more, determined to reach the top. I stopped momentarily to listen to the chirps of a solitary bird in the tree. I recognised the sound – it was coming from the very top canopy. I was drawn to it because it sounded like it was calling out to me. I climbed to the next branch to look for it. It was then that I noticed a Rainbow Lorikeet perched on the highest branch. My father had taught me about these birds and I knew that they travelled in families. They would often congregate in our backyard to feast on the grevillea blossoms. They are noisy and happy birds that are not afraid to come close to humans. In fact, they often called out to us through the kitchen window. So it was odd to see this one all by its lonesome – just like me.

As I climbed closer, it looked at me curiously but didn't fly away. It just kept on chattering, as if it was trying to tell me something. I couldn't help but smile. I reached out to touch it, but it hopped to the nearest branch to reveal the most beautiful bunch of berries that I had ever seen. I picked one and squeezed it between my fingers. It smelled familiar and fragrant, so I ate it. It was deliciously sweet and tangy. At that instant the lorikeet shrieked and flew away towards the hills.

"Wait!" I called out.

My eyes followed its path and my face of disappointment quickly turned into that of relief and excitement. In the distance over the hillside and beyond the tops of many trees stood my home. I yelled out, "woohoo!" I was sure the echo would have been heard for miles.

Instead of climbing down hurriedly to go home, I just stood there on that highest branch looking all around the meadow. I felt strong. I felt wise. I felt free. It was then that I realised that I had found my Garden of Happiness.

Epilogue

Whenever I get lost in life, I remember the Rainbow Lorikeet that guided me home late that afternoon.

I love lorikeets. They are noisy and fun. I keep a picture of one above my writing desk. I look at it often as a reminder of that fortuitous day in the meadow.

I did find my way home later that day. It took a long while to get through the woods and over the hills. Dusk seemed to linger magically for as long as I needed to reach my front door, and long enough to hand me into the open arms of my family.

My falling asleep on that branch made my afternoon walk of adventure seem like it was just a heartbeat from home, when in fact I had ventured a few miles. But that is the nature of adventure. It makes you lose all sense of time. You get lost in the journey. I guess that's what they mean by living in the moment.

It occurred to me much later in life that living in the moment does give you the feeling of being lost sometimes, because it takes you to unfamiliar territory. But is that so terrible? It is life's way of getting rid of distractions so you can focus on the only moment that counts – the present.

Sure, getting lost in those woods was the most terrifying experience of my childhood, but it was also the most memorable and instructive. It led me to discover the eight Trees of my life and taught me to climb them with a powerful pattern of conscious living.

As an adult, I now realise that being lost and not having all the answers is not so bad. It is only when we lose our way that we are forced to take stock of the important areas of life that really matter. Our health, our loving partner, our family's unconditional support, our friendships, our freedom to work and accumulate wealth, the opportunity to learn from great books and great people, and the privilege of helping others whose lives are less fortunate than ours.

I do lose my way occasionally, and it is usually when things are going so well that I take all these areas of my life for granted. But whenever I do, I only have to remember myself in that meadow. I imagine sitting under one of those trees and I ask myself one simple question that always puts a smile on my face. What would that little boy teach me to do right now?

About the Author

Sam Makhoul is a lawyer with over 20 years experience, holding a Master of Laws from the University of New South Wales. He is also an innovative entrepreneur and founder of many successful corporations. He has an intuitive insight into human motivation, developed and refined throughout his career.

Today, Sam is a peak performance coach, speaker and author who is wholeheartedly dedicated to helping people and organisations climb to a higher branch.

Sam is an associate member of the National Speakers Association of Australia and an accredited mentor with Thought Leaders Global.

Sam is also a father of three amazing thinkers who inspire and challenge him daily. Being a loving and supportive father is his greatest achievement.

He lives in Sydney, Australia.

For more information please visit
www.sammakhoul.com
www.ahigherbranch.com

Made in the USA
Columbia, SC
09 December 2020